W9-BHS-693

HE IS RISEN

HE IS RISEN

By

HAROLD PAUL SLOAN

With an Introduction by

BISHOP FRANCIS J. McCONNELL

ABINGDON-COKESBURY PRESS
New York ● *Nashville*

Center for Biblical Studies
51 3777

HE IS RISEN

COPYRIGHT, MCMXLII
BY WHITMORE & STONE

All rights in this book are reserved. No part of the text may be reproduced in any form without written permission of the publishers, except brief quotations used in connection with reviews in a magazine or newspaper.

SET UP, ELECTROTYPED, PRINTED, AND BOUND BY THE PARTHENON PRESS AT NASHVILLE, TENNESSEE, UNITED STATES OF AMERICA

DEDICATED TO

My Wife

Ethel Buckwalter Sloan

WHOSE FAITHFUL LOVE HAS

BEEN ONE OF THE WONDERS

OF LIFE'S ENLARGING

EXPERIENCE

INTRODUCTION

DR. SLOAN HERE GIVES US A FRESH AND VITAL treatment of the resurrection of our Lord. He holds the balance steady between what we call the subjective and the objective phases. Theological thought usually swings back and forth from going too far in one direction or the other in the discussion of the Resurrection. I recall that in the professed explanations I used to hear many years ago, the strictly orthodox theologians would not admit that the body of the Risen Lord was in any respect different from that which was His before the crucifixion. When one such teacher was asked if he could fit such an explanation into the Gospel account which tells that the Risen Christ appeared in the midst of the disciples, the door being shut, he replied that no mystery was involved in the account—Jesus had simply opened the door and walked in.

At the other extreme we have had the interpreters who, if they have made any place for the Resurrection at all, have treated it wholly as a problem of subjective vision, with nothing actually "there." Such explanations have a good deal to say about the wishful thinking of the disciples, about their expecting to see Jesus again after His death, and about the growth of legend, inducing to visions.

Against all this stand these manifest facts: that the disciples were too much bewildered by the events of the Passion Week to be doing effective wishing; that they were not in any expectant mood; that the belief in the Resurrection began before there was time for a legend to start by any such legend-creating process as we find at work in the ordinary course of history.

It is significant that according to the Scriptural narrative the Risen Christ did not appear to anyone not spiritually prepared to receive a revelation from Him. It would have made impressive drama if the Risen Christ could have appeared to Caiaphas or to Pilate, or to Herod, terrifying each with the mistake that each had made. Such a manifestation might have caused terror, indeed, but hardly moral or spiritual conviction. Herod especially was prepared to believe that a man could rise from the dead. He at first thought that Christ Himself was John the Baptist risen from the dead; but Herod was utterly devoid of any power to receive a revelation from the Risen Lord.

The fact that the Resurrection was manifest only to prepared souls is in line with the argument which

Dr. Sloan so cogently presents. The revelations were to spiritually anointed disciples, but they were appearances of the real. We have not material to form any conclusion as to what Paul calls a spiritual body. Paul's own vision of the Risen Christ was overwhelmingly blinding. Perhaps it was well that this was so. The dazzling of the light suggests reality, and at the same time prevents curious speculations as to distracting details. This suggestion of reality back of the appearance is so forceful that a theologian of an earlier generation who interpreted the appearance as spiritual "telegrams" received in vision, conceded that the telegrams were real, coming out of the Supreme Reality, bearing a real message.

It seems to me that Dr. Sloan has kept the balance between the subjective and the objective. The revelations were subjective to subjects prepared to see, and the appearances were of objective reality. The book is the outcome of earnest and devout brooding. Whether it gives final answers to all questions or not, it starts the reader's mind toward productive reflection, which is what such a book should do.

FRANCIS J. McCONNELL

ACKNOWLEDGMENT

THE AUTHOR GRATEFULLY RECOGNIZES THE HELPFUL service rendered by Dr. George W. Henson in reading this manuscript, and his many suggestions for strengthening the message of the volume. He adds also a similar recognition of the service of his daughter, Ruth Sloan Evans.

CONTENTS

The Easter Shout

Vast rending of the purple Easter morn,
Though inarticulate, thou speakest sure:
For, now, no more can death with pall of night
Enshroud the souls of men.   Thy gloom is done!
Thy strength is gone!   The Son of God thy bars
Hath rent!   Look how He bursts thine ancient
   bounds,
And leaping high atop the whole vast frame
Of forces, law, and worlds, cries back to man,
"Behold, O child of fear, thy destiny!"

And us who hear, He bids to lift his cry.
Our praise, the echo of His Easter shout,
He wills to flow redeeming down the years.
'Tis thus through us He binds the broken heart,
And wipes from weeping eyes their scalding tears.
At last He'll be fulfilled; life find its goal;
Creation answer to His promise fair;
Easter become the law; life tower complete;
And man immortal stand, God's utmost work,
Creation's summit, and redemption's crown.

H. P. S.

Easter, 1934

I

The Author's Conviction

THIS VOLUME IS THE RESULT OF A GROWING CON-
viction that the resurrection of Jesus Christ from
the dead is so powerfully certified as to be little
less than a historical demonstration; and that it is
also the very keystone of the Christian arch of
truth.

The central position of the Resurrection is indeed not open to opinions, for The Acts and the
Epistles of St. Paul are conclusive as to its dominating significance in the original Christian message.

This circumstance is striking, and itself has definite evidential value. Jesus' own ministry was one
which gave major emphasis to ethical teaching;
and unless some overwhelming event had taken
place to change things, the apostolic ministry would
have been the same. Yet both The Acts and the
Epistles of St. Paul make the Cross and Resurrection central, whereas the earliest of our Gospels, St.
Mark, preserves hardly any record whatever of
Jesus' immensely important teachings.

Beyond question, then, something tremendous

15

did happen; and it not only aroused the apostolic group out of their despair of Good Friday, but it changed their whole conception of the significance of Jesus. What was this event? Manifestly it was not the Cross, for that event is beyond comparison the most depressing circumstance in history; and the higher you pitch the sublimity of Jesus the more dark the memory of the Cross becomes.

On Good Friday night the Cross was manifestly no gospel. Instead, it was just a ghastly, unbearable tragedy. After the Resurrection, however, this was changed; and the Cross became first a problem, and then an infinite salvation. It became a problem, because when one is known to have died, who has the power to rise from the dead, there must be some explanation of His dying. It became an infinite salvation because the Risen Christ, Himself, taught them that He had laid down His life by the will of God that He might take it again.

There is no room for two opinions with respect to the circumstance that these two events are indeed the center of gravity of the New Testament. Personally I am coming to regard them as the center of gravity of human history. I have no doubt that modern men are just now in danger of losing both political freedom, and every other sublimity of life, because they have allowed these two supreme values to be diminished and called in question. Do you ask, How so? I answer:

Truth belongs neither to man's intellect alone, nor to his aspiring heart alone. Truth can be attained only by complete men, and by men who pursue it in every fact and value of life. It is complete men, laying hold upon the total truth, who are capable of discovering the fullness of life. And manifestly there can be no statement of life which omits anything as immense as the New Testament of Jesus, His Cross and Resurrection. Before Jesus came, civilization, for some reason, lacked the power to make a secure advance. Repeatedly, indeed, it did make a beginning; but always those beginnings failed. Paganism never advanced beyond a certain definite limit. But with the advent of Jesus, and the effective uplifting of Him on a continental scale, civilization moved forward as it never had done before. And the present interruption of this modern advance, itself, further strengthens His evidences: for the contemporary decline of freedom is due to nothing so much as to our neglect and denial of Him. The fact is, the supreme need of the world today is precisely to be repossessed of those life-expanding values which are creative in the New Testament portrait of Him. Human life is in fact one thing if there be nothing larger in history than the records of Cæsar, Charlemagne, and Napoleon; but if history include Bethlehem's Nativity, Galilee's Grace, Calvary's Cross, and Easter morning's death-conquering Son of God, then human life is altogether another thing.

The need of the hour is, thus, for a new depth of intellectual application upon the part of men and women who have become aware of the total dimensions of life. And those total dimensions must include at once its immense aspirations, its tragic failure, and the majesty of the New Testament witness to Jesus and His resurrection from the dead. For this writer, then, the one effort for which our broken, bleeding humanity waits is that *thinking-believing-adoring living* which Protestantism projected into modern times, and which Jesus said was the ceaseless desire of the Eternal Father.

II

The Aspirational Background in Nature for His Transcendence

THE CHRISTIAN CHURCH RESTS DOWN ULTIMATELY upon one most astonishing fact—the fact that the original Christian witnesses did proclaim Jesus of Nazareth to have risen from the dead, leaving His sepulcher open and empty behind Him.

And be it remembered, no observed datum of science whatsoever is more sure than is the fact of this primitive witness. However, speculation may seek to explain this witness, the witness itself is sure beyond the possibility of dispute. Somehow, then, the impression was developed that Jesus' sepulcher did become emptied of its prey, and that He Himself was victoriously alive.

Nor does this amazing declaration stand as the one solitary instance of transcendence in man's otherwise tragically limited history. Christ's resurrection, *as transcendent fact*, stands in striking relationship to man's aspirations, *as transcendent longing*. These two values correspond to and fit each other as a glove does the hand. It may indeed

19

be true that in nature anabolism everywhere gives place to katabolism—life to death; but despite the universality of this process it is equally true that human life everywhere is in revolt against the terrific violence nature, as death, works upon the human soul.

This contradiction in the universe between man's longings and his limiting experiences intrigues one. Says the Hon. J. C. Smuts: "The world consisteth not only of electrons and radiation, but also of souls and aspirations. Beauty and holiness are as much aspects of nature as energy and entropy."[1]

Nature, then, embodies a fundamental incongruity. It has aspirations, but no fulfillment. It has man's majestic life reaching toward the infinite and the sublime, and yet dying. We can indeed steel our being against this contradiction, but it violates us none the less. Even atheism, in spite of its aggressive unbelief, cannot escape from the necessity of the steeled heart. It confronts death with an *unyielding despair*, and this is the best it can do.

Aspiring, dying man—what an amazing contrariety! Yet the facts are quite unescapable: for

[1] *Biology and Christian Belief*, page 42, quoting the Hon. J. C. Smuts's Presidential Address to the British Association, September, 1931, page 14. The author did not use italics.

death is as immense in the universe as a mountain range, and man's aspirational outreach is no less dominating. In history man's aspiration is expressed as magic, superstition, myth, religion, empire, wealth. In literature it is expressed as fantasy, rhapsody, poetry, revelation. In life it is expressed as romance, righteousness, beauty, truth, prayer, faith. If it were possible to exclude from life every expression of aspiration, civilization would disappear, and primitive jungle would again cover the face of the earth. Nor will anyone call this assertion in question. It will be admitted on every hand that civilization is the resultant of man's vast aspirings. What may not be admitted, but what is equally true, is that nature, with its concluding tragedy of death, provides in no respect an answer to man's aspirings. Married love does not fulfill the dream of romance, and even so death does dreadful violence to it.

It is the same with righteousness. Life knows no complete goodness; and once again, the shadow of death is devastating. The fact is, if the tragic littleness of death were not relieved by religious faith, it seems probable it would quite unfound mankind's whole sense of the obligation of ideals. Nor is it any different with beauty and truth. The

quest of beauty inevitably discovers disappoint-
ment, and that of truth, confusion and despair.

In nature, then, man aspires, but he merely aspires and dies. The universe provides no fulfillment for his outreachings. Two courses only are
open to him. He can surrender to disillusionment,
despair, and cynicism, or he can turn from the
natural to the supernatural, discovering the answer
to his need in forces which transcend nature.

There is an incident I heard Professor Curtis
narrate during my student days, which illustrates
the power by which man is urged toward this adventure of faith in the supernatural. There was in
those days, in the city of Boston, a certain well-to-
do and cultured family, a father and mother, a son
and a daughter. The son was feeble-minded. He
grew to maturity a shy, sensitive, retiring individual. He seldom went out of the house; and even
at home he seemed to feel free with no one but his
sister.

Then one day, in the midst of early young
womanhood, the sister died; and the afflicted son
was left entirely alone, utterly desolate.

On an evening before the funeral Professor Curtis called upon the stricken family. He went to
express his sympathy. He was speaking to the
mother. He asked about her suffering son. In

answer she said: "Oh, Dr. Curtis, he is utterly desolate. He refuses to eat. He just sits alone, stunned, brooding." Having said this she was silent for a moment, irresolute; and then she added, "Do you think you would be willing to try to say something to him?"

Professor Curtis went upstairs. She guided him to her boy's apartment. He knocked; but there was no response. He knocked again; then, softly opening the door, he entered. The young man was standing at his west window. The curtains were drawn wide. He was looking with fixed gaze out into the splendor of a New England sunset. Dr. Curtis spoke his name; but he made no response. Dr. Curtis drew close alongside him and spoke again. This time the young man noticed. He responded by pointing out the window and exclaiming, "Over there—over there—she's over there in the glory." He was pointing to the sunset. Somehow that sense experience of brilliant color had become identified in his beclouded consciousness with his intuitive sense of the infinities, and his feeble mind had laid hold upon Eternal Life.

Yes, as I front the New Testament witness to the resurrection of Jesus of Nazareth from the dead, I never face it as just the one amazing exception to the long centuries of humanity's tragic experience of limitation and despair. Rather I always face it as the one place in history where the facts are as majestic as the universal aspirings of the soul. The reach of man's soul is thus the prophecy of Christ's resurrection; Christ's resurrection the fulfillment of the reach of man's soul.

But notwithstanding the striking correspondence existing between *man's universal longing for transcendence*, and the Christian Church's witness to *Jesus of Nazareth and His victory over death*, man's self-sufficient reason tends constantly to be antagonistic. All down the years men have been trying to eliminate Jesus altogether, or to crowd Him within the dimensions of their own inadequate lives; and to explain away His triumph over death. Personally, I am finding this effort increasingly unimpressive. I see it reflecting less of scholarship than of man's choice of self-sufficiency. My own findings can be expressed in three conclusions:

a. Jesus is an historical fact. Quite apart from the New Testament documents, Jesus of Nazareth, the founder of the Christian movement, stands historically indisputable.

c. Jesus, both by the extra-biblical records, and also by historical necessity, was a large figure. No small character possibly could have stood at the center of the Christian movement. Both Socrates and Plato, both St. Peter and St. Paul, would have been far too small.

c. Every record we have concerning Him includes also a witness, direct or indirect, to His victory over death.

The fact is, taking the New Testament as no more than a careful record of the life of Jesus made by sincere men, its accounts of Him constantly confront one with items that transcend all merely human measurements. His thinking, His living, His multiplied cures were all so amazing that the record of His resurrection seems more to explain and justify them than to surpass them.

Take, for example, His teachings. In some of their details, they have been duplicated in contemporary thought; yet in the humility of their mood, the Godwardness of their viewpoint, and the majesty of their sweep, they are quite without parallel. And all these characteristics of Jesus' outlook found their spring in one deeply intuitive experience— *His sense of oneness with the Infinite Father—His sense that He could do nothing apart from the guidance of His Father.* It was the wonder of this one inner experience which explains at once Jesus' teaching and His living. This experience made all life for Him, religion. To walk in the fellowship of His Father, fulfilling His will, and reverencing all finite personalities, was to Him at once religion, ethics, and life.

Nor can there be any question that Jesus actually lived the vision He saw. In Him righteousness was fulfilled. This statement is, indeed, a doctrine of the Church; but it is also a fact of history. The astonishing record is, that Jews, who were almost fanatical in their rigid devotion to monotheism, both accepted this man's life as the revelation of God, and worshiped Him. Nor will any liberties rationalism can take with the primitive Christian documents (except that of arbitrarily rejecting the whole record) get rid of these majestic values. This is the historical Jesus, the only Jesus history knows anything about. His ethical insights dwarf Plato, His religious insights dwarf both Isaiah and Jeremiah. All three of these men, plus Socrates, are morally insignificant by comparison with Him. Jesus is, indeed, constantly an astonishment. He is in fact utterly incomprehensible until at last you see Him victorious over death. It is then, and only then, that you understand Him. It is then, and only then, that you can classify Him in relation to the finite universe, which served as His historic background. No wonder St. Paul wrote nineteen hundred years ago, "Declared to be the

Son of God with power . . . . by resurrection from the dead!"

And now once again I assert that it is both man's right and his obligation, to face this whole tremendous record of the historic Jesus as being himself an aspiring moral personality (not a dying animal). For aspiration is as much a part of the universe as energy or radiation, and to exclude it from consideration is merely irresponsible thinking. If man's faculties had been those of an animal, he would have produced no more science than the animals have: for science, quite as much as poetry, art, and religion, is an expression of man's aspirational life. Shall man, then, whose faculties lift him so high above the beast, deny the actuality of everything those higher faculties need for fulfillment, and shut himself up to the universe of the beasts? And shall he also regard himself as learned and profound because he has done this? Of course the answer is, No. It were more rational to deny all objectivity, as the solipsists do, than to be guilty of such absurdity. Man's aspirations belong to his inner world; and it is this inner world which he knows most immediately, and therefore best. The conclusion is unavoidable: Since man's aspirational powers so greatly influence his outlook upon reality, it is his obligation to make use of them in his explorations of reality. The scientist who might try to do his thinking without making use of his aspirations, would have about as good a chance to arrive at ultimate truth as Michelangelo would have had of carving his Moses with one hand bound behind his back.

Man is an aspiring being, and he has no right to face reality with less than his total equipment. But when with that total equipment he does face the New Testament record, he finds:

That if Jesus' goodness astonishes him, it none the less rejoices him;

That if Jesus' mastership of truth and nature bewilders him, it none the less fulfills him;

That if Jesus' resurrection from the dead overwhelms his natural reason, it none the less is home to his aspiring soul.

III

Faith in Him an Expansive Force Essential to Social Evolution

NOT ONLY IS THE RESURRECTION RELATED TO MAN'S aspirational outreach as the one fact in history which corresponds to and fulfills it; but the Resurrection is also one of the chief creative forces in the ongoing of man's increase toward his individual-social destiny.

St. John voiced this creativity of the Resurrection witness, writing, "This is the victory that overcometh the world, even our faith."[1]   And St. Peter stated the same even more vividly in his noble shout, "Blessed be the God and Father of our Lord Jesus Christ, who according to His abundant mercy hath begotten us again unto a lively hope by the resurrection of Jesus Christ from the dead." [2]

Again and again modern writers have noted the fact that Jesus divides history.   It is true; but why is it true?   We might, indeed, like to think it was because of His teachings; but such a view would

[1] First St. John 5:4.
[2] First St. Peter 1:3.

29

be mistaken. No mere philosophy, however true, ever did or ever will overcome the deep set of human life toward the pettiness of the self-seeking motive. Jesus divides the ages, not because He said, "Resist not evil"; but because He died redemptively and rose again; and because the Holy Spirit is able inwardly to do something tremendous for men and women in relation to precisely these creative facts. Let me put it this way: Bertrand Russell with his ultimate outlook of *"unyielding despair"* never can be the man he might have been had he chosen to share that world outlook which the Christian conviction as to the reality of the Risen Lord produced in the souls of St. John and St. Peter.

Consequently, whether the Christian gospel be true or not, its expansive force, its creative influence, is undeniable. And every department of human interest is filled with the evidences of this fact.

Gothic architecture is but the soaring wonder of Christianity's Easter faith fashioned into stone. Greek architecture was broad, serene, lovely; but the architecture of the Resurrection necessarily leaps skyward.

There is also this same contrast both in poetry and in art. Greek art hardly advanced beyond realism. Greek poetry has no climax grander than

pathos. But Christian art and poetry have wings.
They dare the infinite, visioning even the Eternal
Throne.

One of the greatest stories of history is the account of the reforms the Christian Church produced during the first three and a half centuries of
its existence. Paganism always did, and always
will, do frightful irreverence to personality. Such
an irreverence cannot be separated from its mate-
rialistic viewpoint, and its mood of self-assertion.
Christianity's inevitable reverence for personality,
as such, of necessity came into conflict with this
viewpoint and mood. The Resurrection argued
the imperishable worth of personality; and Christians could not, therefore, be complacent in the
presence of social institutions and customs which
violated it.

The degradation of womanhood, the brutaliza-
tion of childhood, the enslaving of men and women,
the exploiting for amusement of the terrific inten-
sity of death—these and other such practices could
not be accepted with complacency. Here was the
issue: Either the Easter faith had to produce a new
order of society, or that old order of society had to
destroy the Easter faith. The two viewpoints
simply could not remain contemporary and parallel.

The record of history is that faith triumphed—that society was changed.

And now for half a millennium this expansive force of the gospel of the Resurrection has been creative on more than a continental scale. And wherever its witness to the Risen Christ has been carried, there progress has been energized, and social institutions have been transformed. Thus, the gospel of Jesus has promoted political freedom, fostered intellectual advance, been a leaven of social reform, and inspired manifold benevolences halfway around the world. The story is tremendous and the facts are so broadly written that there is no room for dispute. There were no organized benevolences until the gospel produced them. Free government is still wholly the privilege and achievement of Christian men. And very nearly the sum total of scientific discoveries must also be accredited to men who have worked under the expansive influence of the Christian world view.

Paganism did, indeed, achieve a limited advance, and that too along many lines. But it never overpassed certain very definite limits. Thus always its freedoms collapsed for lack of moral undergirding; and its science ever failed for lack of a deep confidence in the universe. Ancient paganism certainly did not have, and modern secularism and atheism have by no means proved they do have the capacity for large and sustained social creativity. Russia's accomplishments are quite largely imitative; and beside, they are but of yesterday. A hundred years from now it will be yet too soon to say with confidence: *Mankind can achieve magnificently, even when its world view is circumscribed by the hopelessness of a limiting death.* Personally I am confident that long before the year A.D. 2017 the Russian people will have reacted from their cramping world outlook or else sunk into barbarism.

I question whether any informed and unprejudiced mind will challenge the statement that the faith of the Resurrection has been expansive in its general influence upon life. But the full significance of this circumstance will be appreciated only when it is stood in the setting of an admittedly evolutionary world view. It is when we conceive the universe as moving to a goal, and the human race as moving to personal and social fulfillment, that the cosmic significance of the faith of the Resurrection will be fully seen.

It is admitted that the remaining stages of human progress cannot be attained by biological forces. Man has made no biological progress in millenniums. Indeed, the cranial capacity of the Cro-Magnon man was definitely larger than that of

modern man. Consequently if the race is to attain
to fulfillment, the remaining stages of man's progress will have to be wrought out at the plane of his
intellectual, moral, and spiritual life. But at this
plane, Jesus is an evolutionary necessity: for history indicates that it is only as men's lives have
been expanded by faith in Him and the Infinite
He made manifest, that they are capable either of
the ideas or of the devotions necessary to fulfillment.

Jesus, then, is a cosmic necessity, if the universe,
as a consistent and coherent whole, is moving to a
national consummation. Mark you, I am not saying that this Christian viewpoint is, therefore,
demonstrably true; but I am saying that you can
develop both a consistent and adequate world view
upon the assumption of its truth. Here are the
essential facts:

a. Human life is evidently a force in unstable
equilibrium. Man is an animal, plus. He is capable
of rising higher and also of falling lower. Which
of these two directions his life actually will take
depends upon his own creative purposings.

b. But which way man will continuously purpose depends to a great extent upon the strength
of the reinforcement he receives to confirm him in
his conviction of the truth of his aspirations. Be-

fore Christ, when the race was without the impact of His sublime revelation, it failed, and that too for millenniums. Again and again it began promising advances, and for a time seemed to make significant increases in them; but at last, and invariably, it failed. Mankind's quest for truth during all that period constantly came out at superstition, skepticism, or just futile fixation; his adventures in freedom consistently collapsed; and his civilizations loitered in failure.

c. Since Christ and the Resurrection, however, and especially since the Reformation,[3] civilization has moved forward with a mighty tread. The reality of Christ's death-conquering life inspired men with confidence in the goodness of the universe, as well as with a sense of the dignity of common personality; and these confidences greatly enlarged them. The results have been manifold. Man has been stimulated in his intuitive drive toward freedom within society; his achievements in this field have been stabilized; his urge toward the discovery of truth has been reinforced with a

[3] At the Reformation two important changes were made in the Church's mediation of Christ's gospel to men. First, worship became truth-centered, the sermon replacing the sacraments in chief emphasis. Second, the gospel became both the possession and trust of the entire fellowship of believers. These two changes vastly increased the effective impact of essential Christianity.

number of sure confidences; and his creativity has been enlarged by his expanded outlook. The consequence of these results has been modern civilization. Christ in His fullness, as effectively given to men since the Reformation, has produced modern history.

Unquestionably a complete statement of the interaction of forces lying behind modern civilization will be much more complex; but it was the confidence He inspired in life and the universe which was most significant. And the truth of this statement is the more manifest now, since our contemporary departure from Christ seems so evidently to be putting a period to progress. For it cannot be denied that we men and women of this day are showing ourselves less effective in self-government than the men and women of 1890 or 1790. Indeed, widely, we seem even to have lost our power to appreciate freedom. What is the explanation? I answer, Modern speculative naturalism has unfounded life. It has made the beauty of Christ and the glory of His victory over death uncertain. It has reduced them to beautiful myths; and it has sacrificed with them all the dignity and promise of life.

Does someone say, I do not accept your interpretation of history? My answer is, I do not ask you to; but I do insist, nevertheless, that it is a possible interpretation. Assuming the Christian gospel, one can see the whole sweep of cosmic ages unified—moving toward a worthy consummation. Katagenetic (running down) evolution is succeeded by anagenetic (running up) evolution; and this at last by the centuries of moral, religious, and social increase. At the end of the way stands the Kingdom of God; and to bring in that glorious consummation God projects into His universe the incarnation, life, death, and resurrection of His Son. In this tremendous event, mankind finds the necessary spiritual reinforcement for moral and social achievement, and history moves forward.

Magnificent possibility!

You do not believe it? Well, you have the other extreme possibility—the "futilitarianism" of Huxley, the "unyielding despair" of Russell! But if you take either of these, remember, your attitude is your personal choice; and its consequence will inevitably work out your own doom.

But returning to that point of view of history we are proposing, let us take time to particularize a little more fully its successive eras and its creative forces. Thus confronted in its vivid details, the reasonableness of our conclusion will be the more convincing.

The first three centuries of the Christian era
should rather be classified among the pagan centuries. From the birth of Christ to the year A.D. 320
Christianity was only a persecuted sect within the
pagan empire. With the victory of Constantine,
and his espousal of the Church, it became for the
first time a world force.

Then during the next seven centuries, from Constantine to Bishop Anselm of Canterbury, the
Church was expanding. It was reaching out widely
to contact in Christ's name the peoples of Europe.

From Anselm to Thomas Aquinas and a little
beyond, the eleventh, twelfth, thirteenth, and four-
teenth centuries, the Church was fashioning its
faith into an established world philosophy.

With the fifteenth century came the Renaissance,
and following it the intellectual, moral, and spiritual tides of the Reformation. Now, at last, Christian truth became the dominant concern of a whole
civilization. Instead of the supra-rational sacraments of the medieval Church, Protestantism came
to men with a preaching-centered worship, with a
Bible in the language and the hands of the masses,
with the right and responsibility of private opinion
in the whole field of truth, and with an entrustment
to the masses themselves for making known the
gospel. Protestantism interpreted Christ's ringing,

"Go ye, disciple all nations," as a command to the whole Christian community, laymen as well as clergy. It should cause no surprise that Protestantism immediately became a movement for general education.

It was in this Reformation emphasis on truth—essentially Christian truth, also, even when it was science—that we have the rise of modern civilization. The Reformation produced a truth-centered civilization; and that civilization inevitably developed freedom, science, and invention. The result was a period creative far beyond all others in human history. The last half millennium from the Renaissance to the first World War accomplished more than all the other millenniums put together.

The world into which Martin Luther was born was one in which any man of any preceding century would have been able to find his way around. Both Aristotle and Abraham, separated from it by two and four millenniums respectively, would have found the main structure of its institutions fully familiar. The fenced cities, the earth-centered universe, the practice of hand manufacturing, the horse as the swiftest means of travel and communication, the absolutist form of government, the use of oil lamps for illumination, the production of books by hand and at great cost—these all were common limitations during all those centuries.[4]

Then suddenly, in the sixteenth century, everything changed. The Renaissance was enriched to become the Reformation. Inspiring truth was given to the masses of men. Almost immediately personality took on new dignity. This universe was indeed the world of God the Father Almighty; and men were His redeemed children, destined in the Risen Christ unto Eternal Life. All truth was inevitably seen as sublime. Men were in possession of that basic confidence without which an increase of science had been impossible. The new reverence for personality, as such, tended also toward a recognition of the dignity of hand labor, removing another of the handicaps which had prevented the continuous development of science in paganism. And so truth leaped forward.

Christian confidence in the universe gave men also a freedom from established political conventions. They sought in nature itself the solution of the problem of government. It seemed to them that under natural law all men had been created free and equal; that inequalities and tyrannies were mere artificialities. They rediscovered democracy,

[4] Printing by movable type, invented in 1428, did not come into general use until the sixteenth century.

and, now, not only democracy, but democracy religiously and morally energized.

As a result of all these new movements, there developed a powerful stimulation of human life which manifested itself in creative thinking and living. Inventions became so multiplied that the years from the founding of America forward stand unique in all the millenniums. It is simply a fact, and indisputable, that from Protestantism's tremendous emphasis upon Christian truth as the chief responsibility and entrustment of men, civilization has achieved more advance than in all the ages before.

How long is history? Recorded history probably dates back to four or five thousand B.C., and yet the last four hundred years have accomplished manifoldly more in social evolution than the sixty-odd centuries which preceded them! What is the force which explains this striking contrast? I answer: The shout of the Resurrection, becoming under the Schoolmen a world view of profound confidence in the universe; the shout of the Resurrection, becoming at the Reformation a supreme and universal devotion to truth; the shout of the Resurrection setting men free, expanding them, energizing them—this is what did it. Of course! A lion in a cage can only do one thing—walk up and down and look for a chance to get out. And what better analogy could we have of the human race as the centuries before Christ knew it? Man shut in by inadequate nature and limiting death was and is just a caged lion. During all the millenniums of paganism man's world view was always too small for him: consequently his achievements were always limited and insecure. He pursued truth, but always came out either at superstition, despair, or skepticism. He achieved civilizations, but always either arrested them in stagnation, or else overthrew them in moral decay and war. This was his record of failure during piled up centuries.

Then came Christianity, and Christianity at last *truth-centered;* and immediately life leaped toward the goal. But alas, we repudiated it for the dogma of scientific naturalism. We degraded high personality to the beast. We became determinists, and mechanists, and futilitarians, until in the midst of a world outlook almost universally degraded there appeared a new and extreme political tyranny. Freedom was on the way out. Spirit had been sacrificed. Truth had been made impossible. Matter and pride of race were dominant. War was inevitable.

Yes, it is precisely thus that sin all down the centuries has been blasting and defeating life. This is the inner self-judgment of evil, because of which it never can arrive at good. The millenniums of pagan failure prove the conclusion. Man without supernatural reinforcement cannot arrive. Jesus and His resurrection from the dead are a cosmic necessity in an evolving world.

IV

The Fact of His Empty Sepulcher

IT IS THE PECULIAR POWER OF THE GOSPEL OF THE Resurrection that it lifts into emphasis a majestic, arresting fact. Because of this circumstance it brings the commanding authority of outward sense experience to the support of mankind's inward spiritual longings. Intuitive spiritual insights, broadly developed, are doubtless a more sure approach to truth than any testimony of the senses; but average men and women do not find them so. Consequently one of the unique superiorities of the Christian religion is precisely that for it the testimony of man's senses do support and confirm the aspirations of his soul.

Aspirations reinforced by vivid powerful facts—that is the peculiar appeal of the Christian preachment. But it always presupposes, of course, that the Christian witness is a solid historical structure.

We start, then, with what must necessarily have been the most obvious of all facts connected with the Christian affirmation of the resurrection of Jesus—the facts concerning the state of His sepulcher

44

during those beginning years of His Church, from A.D. 30 to 70.

Allegedly Jesus was raised from the dead three days after He was crucified; and His Church had a continuous existence in Jerusalem from Pentecost in that year until the city was wasted by Titus forty years later. During a part of this period one of the gospels was circulating, as were also all of the epistles of St. Paul. What then was the condition of the sepulcher of Jesus during those historically significant first years?

Before attempting an answer we need to equip ourselves with a definite picture of Jerusalem and its relation to the Mediterranean civilization. The city itself was a small walled town, about fifty miles southeast of the Mediterranean port of Caesarea. It lay between Alexandria on the south and Antioch on the north, the second and third cities of the Roman world. Jerusalem was thus just off the main travel routes of the day, a city of importance.

It was a mountain city, and exceedingly small. Its walls formed an irregular rectangle, and were less than three quarters of a mile on a side. From the northern gates a main highway led to Damascus; and at this location a new wall was built ten years after the crucifixion of Jesus. Consequently, some

space outside the city in the year A.D. 30 was
brought within its walls by the year 40.

The total area enclosed within Jerusalem's walls
being so limited, the site of the crucifixion, which
lay just outside the north wall, and somewhere between Gennath Gate and Ancient Gate, could not
have been more than a very few minutes' walk
from any part of it. Starting from these gates, it
would be less than three quaters of a mile to either
one of the city's extreme points—the Pool of Siloam
on the southeast, and the Lower Pool of Gihon on
the southwest.

If you visualize this situation, it will become
evident at once that so notable a site as that of Jesus'
crucifixion and entombment must have been well
known during the festival season of the year 30;
and, as a consequence, that the condition of His
tomb on the electric third day after Good Friday
must also have been well known.

Remember, executions in those days were public
spectacles; and that the crucifixion of Jesus was
carried out in the most conspicuous place possible.
Jesus was crucified on a low hill just outside the
north wall, and along the north highway. The
events would thus have been visible from the walls
for 1,800 feet, as well as from the road, and from
the open ground. Multiplied thousands of people

must have seen Jesus die. And the after circumstance of His entombment by two members of the Great Sanhedrin, must have been on the lips of other thousands the next day.

The New Testament record is that He was buried "in the same place where He was crucified"; [1] and the most natural understanding of the words is that the low hill of Golgotha and the garden tomb of Joseph of Arimathea were but a few yards apart. Indeed, since such garden sepulchers were so usually constructed in the side of a hill it would be very natural to suppose that the summit of Calvary was just above the new tomb of Joseph. The expression, "in the same place," lends itself most naturally to this understanding.

Remembering, now, that any story concerning the resurrection of Jesus must have been circulated against the background of what was known to be the condition of His Jerusalem sepulcher, let us note the items included in that early Christian witness.

The testimony is that on the morning after the end of the Sabbath a specific group of women came early to the sepulcher, and upon their arrival noticed that the great stone which had been placed

[1] St. John 19:41.

at its entrance was rolled away; and that the body of Jesus was gone.[2]

St. Mark's Gospel, generally admitted the earliest, and written before the destruction of Jerusalem, preserves this record. It is set down also in St. Luke's Gospel, which, whatever may be its date, was written after St. Luke had visited Jerusalem and the holy sites in the spring of the year 57, or thereabout. St. Matthew's Gospel, in connection with which we have no sure date, knowing only that it was a product of the first Christian generation, and at a time not remote from the year A.D. 70, preserves, also the same.

A closing word at this point: St. Mark's Gospel is usually supposed to have behind it the personal recollections of St. Peter. It is thus the vivid story of an eyewitness. St. Luke's Gospel represents the work of a trained intellect—a man who had made a most careful investigation of the historical data involved. St. Matthew's Gospel, in its narrative sections, is very much less vivid than St. Mark, and very much less exact than St. Luke. It suggests, to any critical reader, generalized information such as would have been current in the primitive Christian community. We have then in the

[2] St. Mark 16:1-9.

synoptic Gospels three different approaches to this central Christian affirmation—the recollections of an eyewitness, the conclusions of a careful investigator, and generalized facts as they were current during those first years.

St. Matthew's Gospel, besides the record of the empty sepulcher, adds two other items which are of considerable historical value. It notes that a guard was placed at the tomb of Jesus some twenty-four hours after He was buried. It notes also that the apostles were accused by the Jews of having stolen the body.

Both of these items did become parts of the primitive Christian tradition; and both of them appear in other writings, Jewish as well as Christian. The Gospel According to Peter, one of the early pseudographic gospels, refused to place in the New Testament, carries this record considerably embellished. Justin Martyr, writing at the middle of the second century, also notes that the Jews unjustly charged the Christians with having robbed the sepulcher of Jesus.[3] The *Toledoth Jeshu*, a violent Jewish attack upon Jesus, also refers to the stealing of the body.

One hardly needs to point out that all these records steadily assume two things: the fact of the

[3] *Dialogue with Trypho*, Chap. 108. 17.

empty sepulcher, and the further fact that this circumstance was a matter of general knowledge.
Manifestly the Jews would not have accused the
apostles of having stolen the body of Jesus except
to explain the evident fact of the empty tomb.
Similarly the primitive story of the sepulcher guard
cannot have been a Christian invention, for as such
it was too poorly done. The story of stationing a
guard, hours after the Saviour's burial, and after
the long hours of an April night had given ample
opportunity for robbing the tomb, is too clumsy
to have been an invention. When liars fabricate
evidence, they never leave such glaring holes.

But if the stationing of the sepulcher guard be
understood as historical, everything is simple. The
Jewish rulers would naturally want to know to a
certainty what happened to the body of Jesus after
His burial; for He had been the center of a vast
amount of wonder, of some intense expectation, and
of not a little venomous hate. From the point of
view of the rulers, the guard was a good idea; but
why, indeed, should the apostles have invented the
story? It could have had no value for them except
as an evidence of the empty sepulcher; and it could
not even have had this value except as the sepulcher
was in fact empty.

There is one more commanding piece of evidence

witnessing to the reality of the empty sepulcher. Jerusalem was destroyed in the year 70, when the Christian Church was forty years old. If tradition be correct, the place of the crucifixon and entombment of Jesus, just outside the walls of the city in the year 30, was brought within them when new walls were built quite some distance farther north, in the year 40. Imagine now a low hill, and near by it a rock-hewn cave, perhaps in the side of that very same hill. There is, indeed, no reason at all why such structureless sites could not survive the violence of an ancient siege. And this would be especially probable if, as tradition says, the new wall had brought them within the city's defenses.

But we have more than probability. There seems to be a definite record that the site of the Saviour's crucifixion and entombment did survive, and that Christians did visit it during the sixty-odd years that Jerusalem lay in ruins. For, when Hadrian was planning the new city, which was to rise above the old ruins, he took pains to violate two sacred spots—the hill of the Temple, and the site of the crucifixion and entombment of Jesus. Eusebius, bishop of near-by Caesarea, and close friend of the first Christian emperor, tells the story in his *Life of Constantine*. I am giving an abbreviated quotation from his account.

Eusebius says that Constantine feels led of the Saviour to erect a monument at Jerusalem in honor of the Resurrection, and then adds: "Godless persons had thought to remove entirely from the eyes of men (the sight of the sepulcher), supposing in their folly that thus they should be able effectually to obscure the truth. Accordingly they brought a quantity of earth from a distance . . . . and covered the entire spot; then, having raised this to a moderate height, they paved it with stone, concealing the holy cave beneath this massive mound. Then . . . . they prepared on this foundation a truly dreadful sepulcher of souls, by building a gloomy shrine . . . . to the impure spirit whom they call Venus, and offering detestable oblations on profane and accursed altars."

This temple, so erected by Hadrian two hundred years before with the alleged purpose of stopping the worship of Jesus there, Constantine orders removed. The pavement is, consequently torn up; the fill of dirt is dug away; the timbers and dirt are carted out of the city. Eusebius then continues: "As soon as the original surface of the ground beneath the covering of earth appeared, immediately, and contrary to all expectation, the venerable and hallowed monument of our Saviour's Resurrection was discovered." [4]

What Eusebius means by "contrary to all expectation" is not that Contsantine was uncertain of the spot, but that he had little hope of finding the "hallowed monument" of Jesus intact after Hadrian's desecration of it, and its two hundred years of burial. When, however, the dirt had been removed, and the virgin rock was uncovered, there was the sepulcher just as Joseph of Arimathæa had loaned it for the burial of Jesus. Eusebius adds that Constantine immediately ordered the erection of a noble structure over the sepulcher to be known as the Church of the Anastasis (Rising). The order was carried out by Macarius, Bishop of Jerusalem; and Eusebius himself took part in the dedication exercises.

We have thus a firm record concerning the empty sepulcher, which starts back during those forty years when the mother church of Christendom still flourished in the Holy City, and both St. Peter and St. James presided over its affairs.

There is, however, a final and unanswerable argument establishing the circumstances of the tomb. It is that, notwithstanding the Christian tradition is quite explicit as to the condition of the tomb; yet

[4] Book III, Chaps. 25 ff.; also Book IV, Chap. 40.

neither Christian preaching nor the official summary of evidences of the Risen Christ makes any appeal to it. Clearly the empty tomb was an admitted fact; but its evidential value was obscured because of the Jewish explanation, which charged the disciples with having stolen the body of Jesus. As a result the Jerusalem church made no apologetic use of this notable circumstance even though every visitor to the city was in a position to see the empty tomb for himself.

How different, indeed, it all would have been had the sepulcher of Jesus remained sealed, and the body of Jesus continued in it! Under such circumstances the Sanhedrin could have silenced the apostles by a simple appeal to the physical facts. They could have produced the mummified body of Jesus and said, "It is absurd to proclaim the Galilean risen, when here are His mortal remains." The Sanhedrin did not do this, but, instead, projected a persecution. The thing is conclusive: for no man ever makes use of intimidations when he is in possession of the most convincing argument of all— vivid facts. I have been in some sharp arguments myself; and I have noticed that men never make use of abuse until they find themselves wanting in information.

Beyond dispute, then, the sepulcher of Jesus is

open and empty, and this is not an item of Christian faith, but a conclusion of history. Men know that the body of Jesus does not rest in the ancient sepulcher of Joseph of Arimathæa in precisely the same way they know the body of Napoleon Bonaparte does rest in the stately Invalides of the city of Paris—unbiased history establishes both. But if Jesus' sepulcher is empty, how was it emptied? Here, indeed, is a quetsion much easier asked than answered.

The libel made use of by the Sanhedrin, of which a tradition is preserved in St. Matthew's Gospel, is absurd upon the face of it. The apostles not only gave themselves unto death in their witness to the Risen Christ; but they gave themselves thus exultantly, and precisely because of their confidence in the Resurrection. There is evidently no possible room for falsehood and self-deception where one is confronted by such an attitude. Manifestly, the apostles did not remove Jesus' body.

But if the apostles did not remove that body, who did? It is equally certain that neither the priests nor the Sanhedrin were responsible. There is an awe of death which would have made any one of those men hesitate to rifle the tomb of Jesus. And even if it cannot be allowed that such motives would have deterred them, still it is certain they did not steal the body of Jesus: for if they had stolen it, they would have had it, or at least have known where they had disposed of it; and such definite facts would have been a far better answer to the apostolic witness than the accusations and persecutions actually made use of. No, and emphatically, the authorities at Jerusalem did not rifle the tomb of Jesus.

Other suggestions are all of them equally absurd. Joseph's gardener has been accused of the deed. But in this suggestion we are again putting the responsibility for the empty tomb within the circle of influence of the rulers: and so long as the rulers either had the body of Jesus, or knew where it had been placed, they would have been in a position to have made effective answer to the apostolic witness.

The soldiers who guarded the tomb have been accused. But here, once more, is developed the same impossible circumstance. If the soldiers had removed the body, the rulers would have known its whereabouts. There is no faintest whisper of such official knowledge. Instead there are just two persistent statements: the apostolic witness to the Resurrection; and the accusation of the rulers that Jesus' disciples had removed His dead body from its tomb.

The suggestion that the women failed to identify

the sepulcher is equally absurd. The Sanhedrin, of which both Joseph of Arimathæa and Nicodemus were probably members, would assuredly have been interested in such a mistake; and we can depend upon it, a correction would have been forthcoming immediately. Then, too, the mother church at Jerusalem could not have continued its activity in that city without the true facts becoming known.

These are the principal suggestions offered by unbelief to explain the empty tomb; and they all alike fail. Three conclusions seem to be securely established:

a. The open, empty tomb of Jesus was a well-known site in Jerusalem between the year A.D. 30 and the year A.D. 70.

b. The libel of the rulers, that the apostles had stolen the body, is utterly impossible.

c. The suggestion that the rulers themselves, directly or indirectly, were responsible for rifling the tomb, is equally impossible.

Manifestly, the most reasonable solution of the historical problem of the empty tomb is just to admit the truth of the apostolic witness. And why not? Resurrection would be but a new creative invasion of the cosmos like that which at another point in the ages had stood organism in the midst of the inorganic, or free, moral, aspiring man in the midst of the animal creation. These creative invasions of the universe were in each instance the beginning of new cosmic forces and laws. At their inception they must have appeared startlingly supernatural; yet, afterward, they both seemed to be, and were, a part of the orderly frame of things. And why may it not be the same with the Resurrection of Jesus? Why may not His triumph mark off a new period in cosmic history, and Eternal Life, the age-old longing of man's race, thus stand at last revealed in Him?

V

Important Dates in the New Testament Witness to Him

Once again we come to dates: and it is dates which chiefly furnish the distinction between myth, on the one hand, and history, on the other. Thus the Buddha stories, the accounts of Lao-Tse, Zoroaster, Osiris, etc., are all doubtless myths because they originated at a date remote from the generations which could have produced history. The Buddha stories come the nearest to a date which would make history possible; but even so they are far beyond the line. Two hundred years after the death of Buddha is the earliest possible date of the *Lalita,* and seven hundred years is the earliest certain date. With respect to all the other writings, the span of years between them and the person whose story they tell, is longer. In some instances the writings are so remote from the men in question that all dates are lost.

In contrast with this, the New Testament accounts of Jesus were all written by men who had had either a personal acquaintance with Him, or else with those who had known Him.

The last writing of the New Testament is St. John's Gospel. The tradition is firm that it was written by the apostle himself, and the internal evidence also is commanding. But even conceding a nonapostolic authorship, very little is lost: for the Gospel, as Archbishop Temple well says, is so intimately dependent upon St. John as to carry a large measure of his authority. This it seems to me is the least that can be claimed: and this makes St. John's narratives of the Resurrection, at the longest, but one mind removed from the work of an eye-witness. Evidently there is not much room here either for tradition or for development.

Definitely earlier than St. John is St. Mark. This Gospel is admittedly, in large part, a second-hand product. It is St. Peter's recollections reproduced by a younger contemporary. St. Mark's Gospel was written before the destruction of Jerusalem, and possibly as much as twelve or fifteen years before.

The next earlier sure date, among the Resurrection documents, is that when St. Luke made the investigation for his Gospel. It was in the late spring of A.D. 57 or thereabout. St. Luke, the traveling companion of St. Paul, was with him during the visit he made that spring to the mother church at Jerusalem. It is explicit that St. James, the brother of Jesus, was head of the congregation at the time. Consequently St. Luke enjoyed three remarkable historical advantages: He had the opportunity of intimate information concerning the Saviour and His resurrection through St. James. He had the opportunity of visiting the sacred sites at Jerusalem. He had the chance to converse personally with many who had seen the Risen Lord. St. Luke, with his definite interest in historical certainty, developed these advantages; [1] and all this wealth of responsible investigation lies behind our third Gospel. Manifestly to use the word "tradition" in connection with such a writing would be about as much out of place as it would be to use it in connection with a mother's recollections of her son's childhood, as retold by him.

But 57 is not the earliest sure date in the record of Jesus' resurrection. In the year 55, or perhaps 54, St. Paul wrote his first letter to the Corinthian Church. In this letter he incorporated a primitive Christian formulary which summarizes the evidences of the Resurrection (I Corinthians 15:3 ff.). He also told the Corinthians that he had presented them with these data two or three years earlier, in 52 or 51. But the formulary itself must have been of a date definitely earlier yet.

[1] St. Luke 1:4.

There are three possible occasions when St. Paul could have received this important statement: upon the occasion of his visit to the capital to attend the Council of Jerusalem in the year 50 (Acts 15:2 ff.); upon the occasion of his visit there after the drought (A.D. 45, see Acts 11:27); upon the occasion of his visit there soon after his conversion, when he spent a fortnight with St. Peter discussing with him the whole history of Jesus (Galatians 1:18).

The earliest of these three dates is clearly the most probable: for it is not likely that St. Paul would have commenced his official ministry at Antioch without first having informed himself as fully as possible concerning Jesus, and especially concerning His risen manifestations. The selection of this first date would mean that the formulating by the Jerusalem church of the chief evidences of the Resurrection goes back very early, perhaps even to before A.D. 37.

Demonstrably, then, there was a formulated statement of the Resurrection evidences, certainly within fifteen, and probably within five years of the event itself. St. Paul was in possession of this synopsis from St. Peter. He was in possession of the details which lay behind it from both St. Peter, St. John, and St. James. St. Luke, the companion of St. Paul, came into direct contact at least with St. James.

Since these things are clearly true, the New Testament witness to the Resurrection has an evident right to be confronted as responsible history. Any other attitude toward it reflects naturalistic prejudice, rather than that scientific openmindedness, which is supposedly characteristic of scholarship.

And let me add, we modern men had better give attention to the moral and social peril inherent in our naturalistic philosophy; for if we do not, that philosophy will destroy us. Speculative naturalism drives as inevitably toward social decay as frosty winds do toward falling leaves. Nature, says William Adams Brown, is the whole field of the predictable—the whole area of experience where forces are constant and consequences are calculable. That is a good definition; and insofar as free personality can be brought within this area it ceases to be personal. Either personality transcends predictable nature or it is not personality. Of course this is as true of God as it is of man. All personal fellowships, whether religious or human, must be experienced at a level transcendent to nature.

The tragedy of modern history is that contemporary naturalism has degraded man to the beast.

It has made us animals. But as animals we are of
necessity dissatisfied; for the animal's limited outlook is too narrow for us. Our speculative naturalism is driving our race into despair; and we must
either repudiate it or accept the tragic descent
which is inevitable.

VI

The New Testament Witness and Its Alleged Contradictory Character

WE CONFRONT, NOW, THE NEW TESTAMENT WITness to the resurrection of Jesus in its concrete details; and in doing so we stand these details against the background of three indisputable facts:

a. Man's universal longing for the infinite—an inner experience to which the outward facts of history make no answer, except in Jesus.

b. The open, empty sepulcher; which was a well-known site in Jerusalem during the early years, at least up to the destruction of the city under Titus.

c. The synopsis of the chief risen appearances of Jesus formulated in Jerusalem, and given by Jerusalem leaders to St. Paul not later than the year 50, and probably as early as 36 or 37.

Before making any effort to appraise this witness, it is important, first, merely to set it down; and immediately it should be noted that this witness is the central concern of the several New Testament writings. Thus, apostolic preaching in The Acts is described as a "witness of the resurrection of the

Lord Jesus" (4:33); and of the various sermons
there outlined every one centers in this fact of the
death and resurrection of the Lord. The one possible exception is the sermon by St. Stephen, which
was interrupted just as the preacher had come to
these matters. But omitting this one, there are
twelve other sermons more or less fully outlined in
The Acts, and their intellectual center is steadily
the passion and triumph of the Saviour.[1]

The same center of interest characterizes also
the Epistles. In Romans St. Paul proclaims the
righteousness of God in Christ crucified and risen
again, available through faith. In First Corinthians
the apostle determines to know nothing among them
but Jesus Christ, and Him crucified (2:2). Ephe-
sians opens with the prayer that believers in that
capital city might know the greatness of God's
power, which wrought in Christ's resurrection, and
which works also in them unto salvation (1:19).

[1] Sermons in The Acts are: St. Peter's on the day of Pentecost (2:14); St. Peter's at the Beautiful Gate (3:12); St. Peter
before the Sanhedrin (4:8); St. Peter again before the Sanhedrin (5:29); St. Stephen (7:2); St. Philip to the eunuch (8:35);
St. Paul in Damascus, where he argues that Jesus is the Messiah (9:20); St. Peter before the centurion (10:34); St. Paul
at Antioch of Pisidia (13:17); St. Paul at Athens (17:22); St.
Paul in the Temple, where he stresses the Lordship of the
living Christ (22:1) St. Paul before the rulers in Jerusalem says
his preaching of the Resurrection is the reason for his arrest
(23:6); St. Paul before Felix (24:10); St. Paul before Agrippa
(26:2).

Colossians contemplates the crucified and risen Christ as being in Himself salvation. When men come into unity with Him by faith and the Holy Spirit, this complete salvation is made available for them, Jews and Gentiles alike. This is the mystery of grace hidden from the foundation of the world, but now made manifest (1:17-27). Hebrews holds the same emphasis, presenting Christ crucified and risen again as the fulfillment of the sacrificial ritual of Israel (compare in particular 10:1-14). First Peter opens with the shout, "Blessed be the God and Father of our Lord Jesus Christ, which . . . . hath begotten us again unto a lively hope by the resurrection of Jesus Christ from the dead, unto an inheritance incorruptible, undefiled, and that fadeth not away" (1:3-4). And First John from beginning to end is a description of the believer's fellowship with the crucified, risen, and living Christ.

This whole emphasis is manifestly strikingly contrasted with the precedent established by Jesus in His own public ministry in Galilee. He preached a high religious idealism. The apostles preached instead a Divinely wrought-out salvation. The contrast, of course, demands an explanation, for apart from some tremendous events the expectation would have been, that the apostles would have continued, if they had continued at all, after the pattern of preaching established by Jesus' own ministry. Yet not only The Acts and the Epistles, but even St. Mark, whose Gospel reflects the preaching of St. Peter, establishes it as a fact that an almighty salvation, not religious idealism, was from the first the chief emphasis of the apostles.

But now, explicitly, what is the primitive Christian witness concerning these majestic events in which this apostolic gospel and preachment took its rise? It begins with testimony to a prophetic fore-announcement by Jesus of His passion and resurrection. And these prophecies are reported as having been both definite and frequent from the early Fall of the Saviour's last year. St. Matthew gives three out of his twenty-eight chapters to an account of those fore-visioned events; St. Mark, three out of sixteen; St. Luke, three (and all of them long chapters) out of twenty-four. St. John is even fuller, giving ten out of his twenty-one chapters to these climatic events.

As to the detail of the gospel record of the death of the Saviour, it need not now detain us. There are definite differences between the several accounts. The Fourth Gospel specifically corrects some misapprehensions for which St. Mark was probably responsible. But all the Gospels agree that Jesus was crucified under Pontius Pilate, died, and was buried, on the eve of the Sabbath during the Passover celebration, probably of the year 30.

Then, on the third day afterward, the immense historical developments began. Early on the morning of the first day of the week a little group of women came to the sepulcher, and found it open and empty. There is complete agreement among the Gospels at this point. There is agreement also that someone within the sepulcher addressed them as they entered, announcing the resurrection of Jesus, and that He would meet His followers in Galilee. St. Matthew notes one angel as speaking to the women. St. Mark notes one young man, probably an angel. St. Luke and St. John each record two angels; but neither of them carries any reference to the general meeting in Galilee, though St. John does preserve an account of a Galilean appearance.

But I am not now interested in detail differences between the accounts. In part the several narratives are clearly supplementary. There are, however, some striking matters of agreement. Thus, there is complete unity concerning the visit of the women; the open empty tomb; the angel or angels who spoke to them announcing the resurrection; the extraordinary character of the Saviour's risen body, which could appear and disappear, and which nevertheless gave the impression not only of objectivity but of tangibility. If it should be pointed out that St. Luke makes Jesus' risen body so corporeal that He could eat broiled fish and honeycomb, it must be borne in mind that the same evangelist makes that body so illusive that He can disappear while men are looking at Him. And St. John presents similarly contradictory data. The Risen Christ appears suddenly in the midst of the apostolic group, as they sit behind barred doors; and yet, having thus come, He is so corporeal that He invites His astonished followers to touch Him.

We leave for a future chapter the discussion of this seeming inconsistency. The important matter, now, is to see that this illusiveness and corporeality is characteristic of the appearances of the Risen Christ generally; and that this is equally true whether we are dealing with the Johannine recollections or the Lukan investigations. A combination of illusiveness and of tangibility characterizes the appearances of Jesus as these were remembered by the apostles and other first-generation Christians.

The arresting power of this witness will not be easily set aside; and we will come to this when we undertake to appraise it: but first it is important that we confront the determined effort of radical criticism to get rid of the whole account by discovering continual inconsistency and contradiction within its several narratives.

These strictures of criticism, while they are intellectually quite irresponsible, are, nevertheless, in part, rather standardized. As presented by one distinguished American critic, they can be summarized in ten paragraphs, as follows:

1. The discplies fled from Jerusalem Friday afternoon, and so could not have been there Sunday morning as St. Luke and St. John say.

2. The structure of Joseph's sepulcher is different in the account in the Synoptic Gospels from what it is in St. John's.

3. The message to the women at the tomb on Sunday morning pointed to an appearance in Galilee, and excluded an appearance in Jerusalem.

4. The appearance to St. Peter, which stood first in the Jerusalem synopsis, is nowhere described.

5. Jesus is reported to have said to Mary Magdalene, "Touch me not," in St. John's Gospel, whereas in St. Matthew's account the women do hold Him by the feet and worship Him.

6. St. Mark describes the women after their experience at the sepulcher as being overwhelmed

into silence. The other Gospels describe them as reporting their experience to the apostles.

7. St. Luke's Gospel describes the Risen Christ as a presence which could appear and disappear; but nevertheless narrates how He broke bread and ate before the apostles.

8. St. Luke, in his Gospel, describes the Ascension as taking place on the same day with the Resurrection, but in The Acts as taking place forty days afterwards. No other Gospel agrees with St. Luke in so compressing the Saviour's risen appearances.

9. St. Paul classifies the vision of Christ which he experienced on the Damascus Road along with the other pre-ascension appearances, so that he at least did not share the physical emphasis in the Gospel accounts.

10. The baptism of the Spirit is reported as having been given repeatedly and under different circumstances. St. John puts it on the first Easter evening. St. Matthew puts it in Galilee, etc. These differing accounts cannot all be true.

Such is the critical assault. It is a forthright attack upon the noblest fact in human history; and yet I cannot remember ever to have read a poorer or more prejudiced piece of reasoning. It is difficult to avoid the conviction that it represents an effort to justify a conclusion which had already been adopted before the evidence was examined. Face, in succession, its ten chief strictures listed above, and their answers:

1. There is quite no suggestion anywhere that the disciples fled from Jerusalem almost immediately after the crucifixion. Jesus' prophecy (St. Mark 14:27), "*All ye shall be offended because of me this night: for it is written, I will smite the shepherd, and the sheep shall be scattered. But after I am risen, I will go before you into Galilee,*" does not warrant such a conclusion. Clearly there was a gathering of the general company of Jesus' followers in Galilee after the Resurrection; but every responsible witness, as well as the natural probabilities of the situation, unite to locate the apostles in Jerusalem at the end, as well as at the beginning, of the Passover-Sabbath of that year.

The arbitrariness of Criticism in this quite unfounded invention of the flight to Galilee would be shocking, if one had not been prepared for it by many similar subjective extravagances of this quasi science. Harnack, Moffatt, John A. Scott, Ernest Scott, C. H. Dodd, Filson are a few of the scholars who, by their own sharp criticism of Criticism, have taught us to accept its conclusions with reserve. Professor Friederich Loofs of Halle, as long ago as 1913 pointed out the complete lack of historic foundation for any apostolic flight to Galilee after the crucifixion. Every New Testament document testifies that the disciples remained in Jerusalem, and that they were there on the morning after the Sabbath.[2]

2. The alleged difference in the description of the sepulcher between St. Luke 23:53 and St. Mark 15:46 is not apparent. The word St. Luke uses is unknown to classic Greek. It is an adjective to which Thayer's *Lexicon* gives the force "cut out of stone." St. Mark's "which had been hewn out of rock" and St. Matthew's "hewn in the rock" both suggest the same idea. But even if St. Luke's adjective does suggest a structure built of hewn stone (which is not indicated), there is no necessary contradiction: for the tomb could not have been cut out of the rock, and finished inside with hewn stone.

3. Admittedly there was an appearance of the Risen Christ in Galilee and probably to a large company of His followers; but this does not exclude earlier appearances in Jerusalem to smaller groups.

4. The synopsis in First Corinthians 15:3 ff. does not say Jesus appeared first to St. Peter, but only that He appeared to him. St. Luke mentions this appearance, and yet fails to describe it. It is quite unwarranted to locate it in Galilee, and so arbi-

[2] Friederich Loofs, *What Is the Truth about Jesus Christ?*

trarily to set aside the only historical information we have about its geography. St. Luke tells us the appearance was reported on the first Easter evening at Jerusalem. Consequently the manifestation must have occurred earlier on that day and comparatively near the Holy City. When radical criticism locates the event in Galilee, or identifies it with Jesus' revealing of Himself to the seven who had gone fishing,[3] it is both arbitrary and irresponsible.

5. The word of Jesus to Mary Magdalene, "Touch me not," could equally well be translated, "Do not lay hold of me," or "Do not cling to me by physical embrace." The command to Thomas to prove His objective reality by touching Him, or the act of the women who held Him by the feet and worshiped, were each different from this act which Jesus forbade.

6. The record concerning the silence of the women after the experience at the empty tomb (not included in some texts), by no means suggests the permanent silence of the women; but merely that their first reaction was one of such fear that they remained completely silent, speaking to no one. Afterwards, they related their experience to the apostles, as all the evangelists assert, and as inevitably they would have done.

[3] St. John 21:1 ff.

7. We know far too little concerning the nature of a resurrection body to be confident such a body could not have possessed the contradictory powers allegedly manifest in Jesus' case. His body seems to have had the power of appearing and disappearing at will, and of disregarding closed doors. Nevertheless it seems also to have had the power of tangibility— Jesus handled physical objects, and was Himself handled by His disciples. In view, however, of the probability that the new physics will yet force science to regard objective things as purely phenomenal, this apparent inconsistency is not too significant.

8. It is entirely unreasonable to assert that St. Luke describes all the risen appearances of Jesus as having taken place in one day. It is quite easy to find two possible breaks in his narrative, one at verse 44, and a second at verse 50.

You do not need to assume a logical break, but only a chronological break, and the Greek *de* is repeatedly used in the Gospels where such a break is almost certain (compare St. Luke 6:39; 16:1; 17:1; 17:22; 21:1; St. Matthew 1:18; 11:2).

Furthermore, St. Luke was intimate with St. Paul; and the latter knew that the risen appearances of Jesus could not have been confined to one day. The five chief appearances listed in the Jerusalem synopsis alone could not have taken place in one day, and this is true quite regardless of their geography.

But St. Luke, himself, makes it explicit that he did not think of the appearances as all having taken place in one day. In The Acts he notes that they were occuring during forty days; and describes the Ascension as an experience in which the apostles were able to gaze after Jesus as he vanished into space. Manifestly such an experience would have been quite impossible if the Ascension had been understood as an event of Easter evening, following Jesus' visit to the disciples in the Upper Room.

9. St. Paul's classification of his own experience of the Risen Christ along with those of other apostles, need not be regarded as arguing the subjective character of the earlier manifestations. Instead the precise opposite may be inferred.

The fact is, the three descriptions of St. Paul's vision of the Risen Christ all suggest that his experience was definitely objective. The vision produced an illumination brighter than the sun, an illumination which blinded him, and one which was seen also by his companions. Evidently no suggestion of anything subjective is indicated.

Manifestly, if Christ's appearance to St. Paul was objective, then the resurrection body must transcend the limitations of space as well as those of matter; but why not? It is certainly a most unintelligent procedure to define things in terms which never were consistent with philosophy, which now are seen to be equally inconsistent with science, and then to make such definitions the basis for a scholarly opposition to the historical fact of the Resurrection.

10. As to the account of the baptism of the Spirit, any casual reading of the New Testament will be likely to confirm the critical objection that there are two markedly differing accounts, one taking place on Easter evening, described in St. John, and one taking place fifty days later, described by St. Luke in The Acts. St. John's is the only Gospel which suggests a time when the Spirit was given; and it may be doubted that his does for it specifically conditions the gift of the Spirit upon the Ascension of Jesus (7:39; 16:7). The account in question involves some highly symbolic action on the part of Jesus (St. John 20:22, 23). The Saviour is pictured as breathing upon the disciples, and saying, "Receive ye the Holy Spirit," after which He commissions them to loose men from their sins.

If this passage stood alone, one would certainly assume it to mark the time and circumstances of the gift of the Spirit; but in view of St. John's explicit statements to the contrary, and the detailed account of the Spirit's outpouring in The Acts, these words of the Risen Christ must be interpreted as a promise rather than as the actual gift of power. Joan of Arc was confident she received several such promises of Divine empowering before the climatic one which set her on her way; and it may have been the same with the apostles.

Before finally passing from the opinions of radical criticism, it is worth while again to lift up a note of warning against classifying it among the exact sciences, or according to its conclusions the authority of science. *Historic Criticism, Form Criticism*, and the newer *Tone Analysis* are all three markedly dependent upon subjective judgment. They are consequently as errant as human judgment inevitably is.

A notable illustration of their lack of reliability is the destructive criticism of the Homeric writings by a number of German scholars. The unity of Homer was denied; writings were assigned to different historic periods; convincing proofs were tabulated. The alleged facts were so impressive that scholarly opinion was widely influenced; the unity of Homer was practically surrendered. Then Professor John A. Scott began a new and exhaustive study of the Homeric writings. He made new tabulations, checking those previously produced. He found the negative critics had been shockingly careless; that they had not even counted correctly. His studies reversed their findings; and his tabulations were so responsibly done that his single volume was sufficient to reverse the trend of opinion, and to re-establish belief in the unity of Homer.[4]

But to return to the New Testament, and to its witness to the resurrection of Jesus—we conclude not only that the New Testament records are not contradictory, but note that several competent scholars have found it quite possible to harmonize them. James Orr, for example, harmonized them in his careful study of the witness to the Resurrection produced about the beginning of this century. His harmonization regards the Matthaean story of Jesus' manifestation to the women in the road as a modified form of that to Mary Magdalene.

Professor Orr may or may not have been correct in this judgment; the fact is, however, that St. Matthew repeatedly makes use of just such markedly generalized material. Indeed, this Gospel is again

[4] This study was made by Professor John A. Scott, until recently of the Department of Greek at Northwestern University. His volume, *The Unity of Homer,* was published just after the first World War.

and again wanting in exact information. Anyone who will compare St. Matthew's narratives with either St. Mark's, St. Luke's, or St. John's will be strongly impressed with this difference.

Not pressing, however, Professor Orr's argument, the following might be set down as a possible harmonization of the Resurrection narratives.

The first appearance was to Mary Magdalene (St. John 20: 11 ff.; compare also St. Mark 16:9).

The second appearance was to the women on the road (St. Matthew 28:9, 10).

Jesus probably appeared next to St. Peter (St. Luke 24:34 and I Corinthians 15:5).

The fourth appearance was to Cleopas and his companion (St. Luke 24:11 and St. Mark 16:12).

The fifth appearance of that first Easter was to the Twelve [5] (St. Mark 16:14; St. Luke 24:36; St. John 20: 19 ff.; I Corinthians 15:5).

The sixth appearance closely resembles the fifth; and is recorded by St. John only (20:24-29).

The seventh appearance was to the seven on Galilee (St. John 21:1 ff.).

The eighth was to a great company, and probably

---

[5] "The Twelve" is repeatedly used to name the apostolic group, not as enumerating the number present on a particular occasion.

in Galilee (St. Matthew 28:16 ff.; I Corinthians 15:6).

The ninth was to His brother, St. James (I Corinthians 15:7).

The tenth was to all the apostles, and is noted in the Jerusalem synopsis and in The Acts (I Corinthians 15:7; The Acts 1:1 ff.).

Facing this New Testament witness to the Resurrection as a whole, we are confronted immediately by several questions. Thus we wonder why so little has been made of Jesus' manifestation to the five hundred brethren at once. This was a most significant event; yet every circumstance connected with it has been allowed to fall into oblivion. We do not know where the manifestation occurred; nor do we know, with exactness, anything else about it. Then, too, we are left to wonder how Christian men could have experienced so notable a manifestation of the Risen Saviour, and yet have doubted, as St. Matthew says "some" did.

It would seem likely that such an appearance to a large group of followers would have taken place in Galilee. This can be inferred because there were more of His followers there; and also because there is such a definite tradition concerning Galilean appearances. The tradition of Galilean appearances is found in St. Mark, St. Matthew, and St. John, as well as in the pseudographic gospels. In St. Mark, strikingly enough, notwithstanding the message of the angel points definitely to Galilee, the appearances recorded all occurred in Jerusalem.[6]

At first thought all this will seem astonishing enough; but it can remain astonishing only to those who do not think a second time. The fact is, it is all exactly natural. The appearances the apostles would have talked about, and recited in their preaching, would of course have been the Jerusalem appearances to small, intimate groups. The *official Galilean* appearance, that to the large company, was such an event as would necessarily have been included in a formal synopsis of evidences; but it never could have become a precious memory, which warm-hearted men and women would have loved to think of, and to talk about.

Criticism quite generally assumes that St. Matthew's Gospel has three sources: a compilation of the sayings of Jesus, the Gospel according to St. Mark, and independent material. Start now with this framework, and imagine a Galilean disciple, who had a general knowledge of the Christian tradi-

---

[6] In nearly all the early manuscripts of St. Mark's Gospel the text ends at 16:8. The ending preserved in our familiar English version is almost certainly an early addition, thought by some to have been written by Aristides in the second quarter of the second century.

tion, combining these factors into a gospel. Such a writer would not put in the Jerusalem appearances with their exact details because he would not know them accurately enough. But he would put in the great Galilean appearance, because, whether or not he had shared it, he would have heard daily references to it by fellow Christians who had been present. As to the "some" who doubted, in all probability they were Galilean disciples of Jesus who had not been present at the great appearance. Like St. Thomas in Jerusalem, these disciples would not believe except——.

A second interesting question is, how does it happen that we have no details at all concerning the personal manifestations of Jesus to the two chief leaders of the Jerusalem congregation? St. Paul had spent two weeks with St. Peter discussing the history of Jesus, and St. Luke himself had talked personally to St. James, yet there is not a line in the New Testament about the details of those two appearances. It was A.D. 57 when St. Luke and St. Paul traveled together to Jerusalem, and so the official synopsis had already been formulated. St. Luke does indeed note that there was an appearance to St. Peter, but he gives no details, and he is entirely silent about the appearance to St. James.

What is the explanation of this striking circumstance?

To begin with, it is entirely understandable that both St. Peter and St. James might have maintained complete silence about their experiences. There are details of my own life in Christ which are too intimate to be shared; and how easily the same might have been the case with Jesus' brother, whose belief in Him was so late, and with St. Peter whose memory of his relation to his Lord included one very great sorrow! Yes, I can understand the silence of those two leaders in the primitive Church about the details of their experience of the Risen Christ. There is, indeed, much in life which will remain secret until everything is at last made known; and how ardently many will wish that some things might remain hidden forever!

But there is an even more amazing reticence in the New Testament. For not only were St. Peter and St. James silent, but the whole Church allowed them to keep their secret. No one undertook by his imagination to fill in this incompleteness in the Christian story. Here, however, reticence is not such, but instead an amazing self-control. It is another evidence of the reverence felt by that whole generation of Christians for the "Precious

Deposit" [7] which had been entrusted to the apostles by the Saviour. The first Christians evidently felt that the fact of Christ was a Divine revelation too sacred even for an adoring imagination to add to it.

Nor does one need to read long in the non-canonical literature, afterward produced in the Church, before this self-control of that first generation will be seen to have immense evidential significance. Those later works, produced after the restraining authority of the apostles was removed, give most free play to the imagination. Their narratives are constantly encumbered, and frequently distorted by pious falsehoods. The writers, doubtless, meant to glorify Jesus. What they did was to make Him fantastic, and at times even diabolical. A little later on we will have to make rather a careful examination of this third and fourth generation Christian literature. For the present, however, we only note that it contrasts strikingly with everything in our New Testament. Unquestionably the first Christians were deeply impressed by the importance of their trust, and guarded it sacredly.

In bringing this division of our discussion to a close, it is important to notice two additional facts: First, while the Jerusalem synopsis of the evidences

[7] II Timothy 1:13.

of the Resurrection (preserved by St. Paul in I
Corinthians 15:3 ff.) gives no geographical indenti-
fications, yet the appearances of Jesus it catalogues
do fit perfectly into the third, fifth, eighth, and
tenth appearances as compiled above. Second, both
St. Matthew and St. John record appearances of
the Risen Christ in Galilee as well as in Jerusalem.
St. Luke, whose narratives all concern Jerusalem,
probably omitted Galilee because of the superior
definiteness of the Jerusalem details; and possibly,
also, because of his better opportunity for making
investigations in Jerusalem than in Galilee.

VII

An Appraisal of the New Testament Witness

WE NOW ARE IN POSSESSION OF SEVERAL SURE AND
approximately exact dates connected with the New
Testament witness to Jesus. We have achieved
also a general understanding of the main outline of
events. We now need to make a careful appraisal
of the responsibility of the witnesses in question,
and of the worth of their testimony.

The natural place to begin this most significant
study is, of course, with that Jerusalem synopsis
of data to which already we have referred. Writing to believers at Corinth, St. Paul tells them that
he began his ministry among them by preaching a
body of data he, himself, had received. He then
incorporates the Synopsis:

*Christ died for our sins according to the Scrip-
tures; and He was buried. He rose the third day
according to the Scriptures: And he was seen of
Cephas, then of the Twelve. After that, He was
seen of above five hundred brethren at once; of
whom the greater part remain unto this present, but*

*some are fallen asleep.   After that, He was seen of
James; then of all the apostles.*[1]

This official list of appearances by St. Paul could
not have been received later than the year A.D. 50,
the date of his latest visit to Jerusalem before his
ministry in Corinth. The probability is he received
them definitely earlier than A.D. 50.   But no matter
when the formulary itself was conveyed to him, the
facts recited in it must have been taught him upon
the occasion of his visit to St. Peter directly after
his sojourn in Arabia.   St. Paul himself makes a
reference to this two-week period in Galatians.[2]

Involved in these details of history is a truth the
evidential value of which cannot be exaggerated.
It is that St. Paul's personal contact with the chief
evidences of the Resurrection was through eyewitnesses.   Of the appearances of Jesus listed in the
official synopsis, St. Peter himself took part in two
of them, and probably four; whereas St. James took
part in one of them, and probably three.   In addition St. Paul conversed with both St. Peter and St.
James at Jerusalem, and received from them at first-
hand accounts of the appearances of Jesus as each
had experienced them.   The conclusion is not only
that the information underlying St. Paul's preaching

[1] I Corinthians 15:3 ff.
[2] Galatians 1:18.

was directly received; but also that the Jerusalem Synopsis, itself, was a compilation of first-hand evidences not made later than A.D. 50 and probably as early as A.D. 35.

After the Jerusalem Synopsis our next most important writing is the Gospel of St. Luke; and it is interesting to note in part an identity of order between it and the Synopsis. When Cleopas and his friend had gained admittance to the Upper Room on the first Easter evening, the apostolic group greeted them with the shout, "The Lord is risen indeed, and hath appeared unto Simon." Immediately following this greeting, so the Lukan narrative reads, Jesus made Himself manifest to "The Twelve." Consequently in the third Gospel, as well as in the Jerusalem Synopsis, the order of events is, "He appeared to Cephas; then to The Twelve." [3] The Fourth Gospel, also, has an account of the manifestation of Jesus to the apostolic group on the first Easter evening. The familiar ending of St. Mark's Gospel, as printed in the King James Version, is admittedly not a part of the original Greek text. It is, however, an early addi-

[3] "The Twelve" is evidently used as an official designation of the inner apostolic group, and not as a count of those present, for not only was St. Thomas absent, but Judas was dead. The Markan ending in fact substitutes "The Eleven" for "The Twelve."

tion; and it is significant that it, too, carries an account of that first manifestation of Jesus to "The Twelve."

The primary, first-hand testimony preserved by St. Paul, being a synopsis of evidence only, carries no details; but this is not the case with respect to the supporting testimony recorded in the third and fourth of the Gospels. St. Luke's own witness to these facts cannot have been more remote than third hand—St. Peter through St. Paul—and it may even have been second hand; whereas that of the author of the Fourth Gospel was, at the remotest, second hand—St. John through another. St. Luke tells us definitely that the purpose behind his gospel was to make a careful check of the historical reliability of the Christian tradition; [4] and the well-known responsibility of this author's historical studies entitles his testimony to most respectful consideration.

The Jerusalem Synopsis, even standing alone, is a most significant document; but when one remembers that it is supported by St. Luke's investigations made at Jerusalem in the year A.D. 57, and the personal recollections of St. John, it becomes definitely more challenging. But even this powerful body of evidence by no means exhausts the historical data

[4] Compare St. Luke 1:1-4.

preserved in the New Testament. There are in fact some thirty different items of evidence recorded there. Some of these are equally direct and impressive with those already mentioned. Others are quite remote, and of much less significance. However, the very volume of this testimony makes necessary some event large enough to have produced it: for it would have been impossible to have developed so great a mass of records without some facts.

It will be helpful, quite without discussion, just to list this mass of material. Roman numerals will be used for the separate items, Arabic numerals for the individual records, and bracketed characters to evaluate their worth in each instance. Testimony by an eyewitness will be marked (1), secondhand (2), more remote, but still direct (D), dependent upon another writing (d), and general Christian knowledge or tradition (T).

I THE EMPTY SEPULCHER AND THE ANGELIC MESSAGE

1—St. Matthew 28:1-8 (d) plus (T)
2—St. Mark 16:1-8 (D) and possibly (2)
3—St. Luke 24:1-11 (d) plus possible (2)
4—St. Luke 24:22-23 (D) possibly (2)

II The Empty Sepulcher Investigated
      5—St. John 20:1-10 (2) perhaps (1)
    [5] 6—St. Luke 24:12, 24 (D) perhaps (2)

III The Setting of the Watch, Etc.
      7—St. Matthew 27:62-66 and 28:11-15 (T)

IV The Appearance to Mary Magdalene
      8—St. John 20:11-18 (D) perhaps (2)
      9—St. Mark 16:9-11 (T) and perhaps (D)

V The Appearance of Jesus to the Women on
      the Road
      10—St. Matthew 28:9-10 (T)

VI The Appearance to Cleopas and Companion
      11—St. Luke 24:13-32 (D) perhaps (2)
      The repeated similiarity between St. Luke
      and The Fourth Gospel suggests the possi-
      bility that St. Luke had conversed with the
      Beloved Disciple.
      12—St. Mark 16:12-13 (T)

VII The Appearance of Jesus to St. Peter
      13—St. Paul in I Corinthians 15:5 (2)
      14—St. Luke 24:33-34 (D) and perhaps (2)

VIII The Appearance of Jesus to the Twelve
      15—St. John 20:19-23 (2) and perhaps (1)
      Both this record and that of IX lack the vivid-
      ness of St. Luke's account, or of St. John's
      record of II or IV above or X below.

[5] St. Luke 24:12 is classified as a very early interpolation in
Nestle's text, which is dependent on Westcott and Hort,
Tischendorf, and Weiss.

16—St. Luke 24:36-49 (D) and perhaps (2)
17—St. Mark 16:14-18 (T) and perhaps (2)
18—St. Paul I Corinthians 15:5 (2)

IX THE APPEARANCE OF JESUS TO THE TWELVE, AND
    ST. THOMAS
    19—St. John 20:24-29 (2) and perhaps (1)

X THE APPEARANCE OF JESUS TO THE GROUP ON
    GALILEE
    20—St. John 21:1-22 (2) and perhaps (1)

XI THE APPEARANCE OF JESUS TO THE FIVE HUNDRED
    21—St. Paul in I Corinthians 15:6 (2)
    22—St. Matthew probably 28:16-20 (T)

XII THE APPEARANCE OF JESUS TO ST. JAMES
    23—St. Paul in I Corinthians 15:7 (2)

XIII THE APPEARANCE OF JESUS TO ALL THE DISCIPLES
    24—St. Paul in I Corinthians 15:7 (2)
    25—St. Luke 24:50-53 (2). The identification
        of this appearance with that recorded also
        in The Acts is highly probable.
    26—The Acts 1:4-9 (D) and perhaps (2)
    27—St. Mark 16:19-20 (T) and perhaps (2)

XIV THE APPEARANCE OF JESUS TO ST. PAUL ON THE
    DAMASCUS ROAD
    28—St. Paul in I Corinthians 15:8-9 (1)
    29—The Acts 9:1-9 (2)
    30—The Acts 22:6-11 (2)
    31—The Acts 26:12-15 (2)

Evaluating this testimony, we find the empty
sepulcher is certified both by the direct witness of

St. Peter, and also by the women, whose experience was reported by St. Peter. St. Luke later checked for himself the facts, during his visit to Jerusalem in the year A.D. 57. We have thus at least three lines of independent testimony, even without making any use of the Johannine record.

The apostolic examination of the sepulcher, in the Fourth Gospel, is convincingly that of an eye-witness. The Lukan reference to it, in the account of the two going to Emmaus, is also so vivid that one wonders if Cleopas, himself, was not St. Luke's source.

The account of the setting of the watch, in St. Matthew, probably reflects an early tradition. It was a well-known fact, but of definitely more importance in Galilee than it could have been in Jerusalem.

The narrative of the appearance to Mary Magdalene is so vivid that one feels confident the responsible author must have heard her tell it. The reference to it in the Markan ending demonstrates that it had become a part of the primitive tradition.

The Matthean account of the appearance to the women on the road is thought by the conservative scholar, James Orr, to be a modification of the appearance to Mary Magdalene. In view of this Gospel's frequent use of current tradition as a source, the suggestion does not seem improbable.

The account of the fourth of the Easter manifestations is one of the loveliest and most evidently historical of the entire series. We have already referred to the possibility that Cleopas might have been St. Luke's source. The difficult circumstance of the "holden eyes," and the fact that the Saviour, who disappears while they are looking at Him, yet eats bread before them, is just the kind of a record the author of our third Gospel never would have made, except his sources had forced it upon him.

The appearance to St. Peter, we have in direct testimony in the Jerusalem Synopsis, and also in indirect testimony through Cleopas and St. Luke.

The appearance to the Twelve on the first Easter evening in the upper room is supported by four independent records, as follows: The testimony of the Fourth Gospel, the indirect testimony of St. Peter through St. Paul, the indirect testimony of St. Peter through St. Luke (perhaps as mediated by St. James), and the still more indirect testimony of the Markan ending, in which account the incident has become tradition.

The special manifestation to St. Thomas is re-

ported only in the Johannine narrative, which repeatedly preserves details about St. Thomas.[6]

The very beautiful story of the appearance to
the fishing party on Galilee is something rich beyond the possibilities of tradition, and restrained beyond the possibilities of imagination. Evidently we
are dealing with a burning memory written by some
one who has touched a first-hand testimony.

The appearance to St. James is first-hand testimony through the Jerusalem Synopsis. The fact
that this notable item of evidence is not reflected
in the primitive tradition makes even more certain the first-hand nature of our source.

The final appearance, to all the apostles, is certified at first hand in the Jerusalem Synopsis, and by
direct testimony through St. Luke in The Acts.
Its inclusion also in one of the Markan endings
shows that it did get into tradition.

The account of the post-ascension appearance to
St. Paul comes to us as both first- and second-hand
testimony. The acceptance of St. Paul by the other
apostles shows that the objectivity of his experience was recognized by them: for one of the essential marks of an apostle was to have seen the
Lord.

Confronting this array of evidence, one is im-

[6] Compare St. John 11:16; 14:5, etc.

mediately aware of the remarkable circumstance
that it is very largely independent of any legitimate question of Criticism. The Jerusalem Synopsis is first-hand evidence, and exceedingly early.
St. Luke's contacts with the primitive data through
St. Paul and St. James, and probably also St. Peter,
St. John, and others of the inner circle, is in no way
involved in the discussion as to whether his Gospel
was written in A.D. 60, 70, 80, or 90. But more
significant still, the fact that so much of its testimony, as it has come to us, is either first or second
hand, lifts it quite out of the sphere of critical
discussions. The recollections of eyewitnesses are
not greatly influenced by the repetitions which
result in tradition. Professor Filson has pointed
this out most emphatically in his recent discussion
of the origin of the Gospels, saying, "Folk tales do
not reckon with eyewitnesses. Form Criticism also
tends to forget them. . . . In contrast with this serious fault . . . we must hold that the eyewitnesses
mentioned in St. Luke 1:2 exercised a great control over the tradition in its early and crucial
stages." [7]

So much for the various records of the Resurrection—what now of the Gospels in which they are
embedded? The first Gospel, that by St. Mat-

[7] Filson, *Origins of the Gospels,* p. 107.

thew, is generally supposed to be dependent upon an original collection of the teachings of Jesus, plus our second Gospel. Its additional material, much of it, very much generalized, and some of it, even blurred, would be best understood if it were regarded as a product of those oral narratives in circulation in the churches from the very beginning. Bishop Quadratus of Athens at the opening of the second century gives a vivid picture of the constant repetition of both the words and works of Jesus which constituted a central feature of Christian worship. Such oral tradition would lack the vividness of the eyewitness, and the exactness of the product of an investigator; but it would have, nevertheless, its own definite evidential value.

St. Mark's Gospel, the earliest to be written, admittedly touches first-hand information through that evangelist's contact with St. Peter. St. Mark wrote the story of Jesus as he had heard St. Peter narrate it in sermons; and there is hardly a chance that the latter's vivid recollections would be modified by the influence of rhythmic sentences or repetitions connected with primitive worship. These suggestions of contemporary Form Criticism have but little significance when one is dealing with the recollections of immediate experience.

St. Luke, the author of our third Gospel, has been rated a most reliable investigator by both Adolph Harnack and Sir William Ramsey, to mention only two. His intimate contacts with St. Paul, and those exceptional opportunities for study connected with his visit to Jerusalem in the year A.D. 57, give to his Gospel and The Acts exceptional historical value. It is practically sure that St. Luke did meet St. James, the head of the Jerusalem congregation, during his visit to that place; and it is possible that he may have met both St. Peter, St. John—yes, even the Virgin.

The two latter of these possibilities intrigue one. There is a marked agreement between the third and fourth of our Gospels, and yet any possibility of interdependence between them is well-nigh impossible. Take some details. Both of these Gospels note that it was the right ear of the high priest's servant which St. Peter cut off. They both note that Jesus was accused before the governor of a most serious charge, and that Pilate formally acquitted Him. Both, again, record two (rather than one) angels at the empty tomb. Both include some notation as to an apostolic investigation of the sepulcher.[8] Finally, both carry an account of Jesus'

[8] Even if St. Luke 24:12 be an addition to the text, 24:24 preserves a record of the same circumstance.

Center for Biblical Studies
51 3777

manifestation to "The Twelve" on the first Easter evening. This notable agreement raises the question, whether St. John may not have been in Jerusalem when our third evangelist came there in the spring of 57, and if he may not have assisted in his study of the tradition of Jesus. The probability of this circumstance is increased by the marked Hebrew style of St. Luke's narrative of the Annunciation and the Nativity. If St. Luke actually had heard either St. John or the Virgin relate those simple, sublime narratives, one could understand why even their Hebrew structure reappears in his telling of them.

Finally, coming to the Fourth Gospel, we find in it an exactness of detail, which repeatedly clarifies, and at times even corrects the accounts of the other evangelists. This circumstance powerfully suggests the eyewitness; and tradition is substantially unanimous that the Beloved Disciple was the author. Much contemporary criticism is opposed to this conclusion; but as Archbishop Temple has well said, the least that can be claimed is that St. John was the responsible authority behind the Gospel which bears his name.

When one remembers that the Fourth Gospel did not appear until the others had been fully established, and then confronts its completing and cor-

recting details, one's sense of an apostolic source
becomes little short of compelling. Take a few
of these items. The Fourth Gospel records a
cleansing of the Temple at the beginning of Jesus'
ministry, and a period of public activity in Judea
between His temptation and the imprisonment of
John the Baptist. It corrects the time of the anoint-
ing at Bethany, and the nature of the supper Jesus
ate on Thursday evening with the Twelve (moving
up the Passover, proper, from Thursday-Friday
to Friday-Saturday). It improves the record of the
giving of the sop, of the prophecy of St. Peter's
denial, of the dividing of Jesus' garments, and of
the entombment.

Then in addition, the marks of the eyewitness
are almost constant upon it. One is impressed that
it would take a most powerful argument, or else
a more powerful prejudice, to set aside this Gospel's
evident indications of precise care, and vivid recol-
lection. The internal evidence of apostolic authority for the writing is convincing. Only by
resolute effort can one escape the conviction that
this noblest of the accounts of Jesus has behind it
the burning memories of St. John the Divine.

Contrast for a moment the impressions made by
a reading of the independent narrative sections of
St. Matthew, or even of St. Luke, with those of

the Fourth Gospel. St. Matthew is blurred and generalized, as if its source had been current general information. St. Luke is not blurred, but does lack vividness. It is clearly the work of an investigator. But the Fourth Gospel is repeatedly vivid, and rich also in intimate recollections which have no particular significance except to the one who remembered them.

Here, then, are four viewpoints, all of them coming out of the first century; all of them, also, coming out of intimate contact with the first Christian generation. Two of them stand so close to the inner circle, and to eyewitnesses, that they demand the very first rating as evidential documents. Of the other two, the first reflects the current Christian tradition then circulating in the churches, and the other the careful investigations of a competent intellect made on the ground, and during the lifetime of the first Christian generation.

All four of these documents, notwithstanding their wide divergence of viewpoint, portray one majestic figure—

One who knew Himself to speak with the authority and finality of the Living God;

One who even stood Himself beside the Living God, as sharing the devotion of men;

One who, having died redemptively, was raised from the dead to be the Saviour of men.

And so a brooding mystic, a man of impulse and action, a careful investigator, and a narrator of common report—all four agree with respect to the salient facts about Jesus. The New Testament authors are thus seen to have known but one august Personality—one hope of Eternal Life. And to this single value they all bear witness with a solidity of conviction which cannot be shaken, and with a restraint which cannot be tempted to extravagance.

VIII

Galilee and the Pseudo Gospels

NEGATIVE CRITICISM HAS REPEATEDLY STRESSED Galilee as the center from which the gospel of the Resurrection spread; and it has done this notwithstanding the fact of a powerful emphasis in the New Testament pointing to Jerusalem. The detail of this latter emphasis might be summarized as follows:

1. The testimony of St. Luke, which has as its basis investigations made by him in Jerusalem in the late spring of 57. St. Luke records four Jerusalem appearances: (*a*) that to Cleopas and a friend; (*b*) that to St. Peter; (*c*) that to the eleven on the first Easter evening; (*d*) that to the whole company of the disciples upon the occasion of the Ascension.

2. The testimony of our First Gospel, which develops the general Christian understanding of the events rather than exact information. Such an absence of exact information is repeatedly characteristic of the First Gospel in its narrative sections. Again and again St. Matthew seems to have

been satisfied just to report general circumstances, and not to have been interested in precise details. Nevertheless, notwithstanding, he stresses a Galilean appearance of the Risen Jesus, he includes also an account of a previous manifestation at Jerusalem early in the morning on that first Easter Day.

3. The testimony of the Fourth Gospel, which certifies to three appearances taking place at Jerusalem: two on the first Easter, and one on its next weekly anniversary. The closing chapter of the Fourth Gospel notes also one, and may suggest a second Galilean appearance of Jesus.

4. The testimony of the longer Markan ending, which definitely notes one Jerusalem appearance on Easter morning. It is to Mary Magdalene. The other geographically unidentified appearances specified in this ending may well be two of the four of which we have the details in St. Luke. Indeed, unless we greatly multiply Jesus' Risen manifestations, this must be the case.

5. The testimony of the Jerusalem Synopsis, preserved by St. Paul (in I Corinthians 15:3 ff.). And here again, unless we multiply appearances, we are dealing with St. Luke's second, third, and fourth, as listed above.

The weight of this evidence points powerfully to Jerusalem. Indeed, it is impossible, except by

violence, to set this testimony aside. But this is
not the whole of the story. In addition to St.
Matthew's Gospel, which definitely affirms an appearance in Galilee, the same is to be inferred both
from the message of the angels to the women in its
Markan form, as well as from the firm tradition developed in the several pseudo gospels—The Gospel
according to Nicodemus, The Gospel according to
Peter, etc. St. John also includes an account of
at least one Galilean appearance of Jesus.

Every Gospel in our possession, then, with the
exception of St. Mark, of which the last verses
have been lost, affirms at least one Jerusalem appearance of the Risen Christ; but St. Matthew, and
pseudo Nicodemus, and Peter put no emphasis
upon these appearances. Their stress is constantly
upon our Lord's manifestations in Galilee. What
is the explanation of this shifting of the emphasis?

When first I became aware of the circumstance,
it seemed to present real difficulty; but the more
I thought about it, the more natural it came to
appear. Jesus, it must be remembered, had many
hundreds of adherents in Galilee. Numbers of
these people were not His committed followers.
They were, nevertheless, interested in Him, and
inclined to appreciate Him. Among this larger
company was also a closer group, amounting to

around five hundred, to whom Jesus showed Himself alive from the dead.

In Galilee, therefore, there was a considerable body of people who were both interested in Jesus, and who talked about Him. Imagine, now, some of these peripheral disciples hearing over and over again, day after day, accounts of His great risen manifestation there in Galilee. Those accounts would run somewhat as follows: "I was there upon the mountain, where we had been told to assemble. I was sitting on the grass conversing, when suddenly some one said, 'There's Jesus!' and we saw Him approaching, walking in the midst of a small group of His intimate followers." Suppose you had shared such a close contact with the Risen Christ; and then suppose afterward, you had heard indirectly of appearances of Jesus which were reported to have taken place far away in Jerusalem to St. Peter, etc.—which one of the two experiences would have made the vivid impression on your mind? Which would you have been most apt to have talked about?

There is no need to answer. Quite apart from the circumstance, that the more intimate manifestations were bound to be more significant as the years went by, the large experience that you yourself had heard talked about first hand, and again and again, would be the one you would dream about, and that you would put into any account of Jesus you might be writing or amending. And so it happened that there was a dominant tradition about the Galilee appearance or appearances, and so, too, it happened that Galilee was the source of so much of that imaginative material which is preserved for us in the pseudographic gospels.

But one should not pass from these gospel fictions, several of which are comparatively early, without taking note of one remarkable difference between them and the canonical accounts. The Protoevangelium of James, The Gospel of Thomas, and The Gospel of Peter were all three almost certainly in circulation during the lifetime of Justin Martyr—the third Christian generation. Yet a comparatively free used of the imagination is manifest in all of them. Thus, again and again, we come upon fantastic circumstances which simply could not have been true; and there are even circumstances where the uses made of the supernatural in these gospels are definitely immoral. This is, indeed, a most marked contrast to the records preserved in our New Testament, where there is not one act narrated of Jesus which could cause the most sensitive conscience even one pang of regret.

But instead of discussing them, take some concrete instances of their immoral imaginative material. The Gospel of Peter is one of the very earliest of these pseudographs; and yet there are numbers of imaginative extravagances in it. Thus the earthquake which took place in connection with the death of Jesus is timed to have occurred at the precise instant when His hands, having been released from the cross, touched the ground. Or again, the Resurrection is seen by the soldiers as a most marvelous spectacle. The heavens open. Two angels sweep from the cleft skies down to the tomb. They enter; and then in a moment they come forth again, accompanied by a third person, whose head reaches above the heavens. Coming out of the tomb in the train of these three is a cross, which has the power of speech; and when heaven inquires concerning Jesus' activity during His entombment, this cross makes vocal answer.

The Gospel of Nicodemus allows even greater freedom to the imagination. The imperial standards make obeisance to Jesus as He enters Pilate's judgment hall; and they do this a second time, when men of the greatest strength have been put in charge to prevent it. Joseph of Arimathea is imprisoned by the Jews for burying Jesus. But after our Lord is Risen He lifts that prison house quite clear of its foundations and, entering in, brings Joseph out.

Then He conducts Joseph to the empty sepulcher to prove the reality of the Resurrection.

Later, Phineas, a priest, Adas, a teacher, and Haggai, a Levite, come to Jerusalem from Galilee to report to the rulers that Jesus has been seen in Galilee along with His followers on Mount Mamilch (the designations of these men and of this mountain vary markedly). The result of these reports, together with that of Nicodemus and Joseph, is that the rulers are moved to repentance and at least to a degree of faith.

But turning from these more mild expressions of imagination in the earlier of the pseudographic gospels, and picking some which are later, we find a most amazing increase of imaginative material. Some of this is, indeed, not lacking in artistic power; though most of it is at once both crude and fantastic.

The Protoevangelium of James in particular incorporates some very beautiful material; though even so, it is definitely fantastic. Take, for example, the account of the Saviour's birth. Joseph is approaching the cave of the Nativity, where he had left Mary when he had gone in search of a midwife. As he approaches he becomes aware of a luminous cloud encompassing the cave. Then after a moment he sees the cloud become a radiance within the cave. The whole inside of the grotto becomes intensely brilliant; and, even as he watches, the brilliance is transformed into the Child Jesus, resting upon His mother's breast.

According to this description nearly every resemblance to human birth has been removed from the incarnation process. Indeed the realism of Mary's having carried the Child continues only as an abnormality. Jesus is less *born* than *appears*. The solid reality of the New Testament is replaced by fantasy.

But there are items yet more fantastic, and much less artistic. Elizabeth and John the Baptist are fleeing from the wrath of Herod. They can find no avenue of escape. In desperation the mother cries to the mountains to protect her, and immediately the face of one of them opens up and receives her. Zacharias, however, is not so fortunate. Herod murders him at the altar; and later, when the priests find his body, his shed blood has turned to stone, and the fretwork of the sanctuary makes a wailing lamentation over him.

The Gospel by Thomas is still more fantastic. Jesus is described as a little boy playing in Nazareth. He makes Himself pools with tiny dams, and then molds mud into toy birds. These He flings into the air, and transforms them into living things.

They fly away singing. The son of Annas breaks down the dams, letting the water flow away; and Jesus, furious with anger, curses the boy, who immediately withers and dies. Similar fatalities occur so frequently that Joseph is afraid to have Jesus go out of the house, lest the people come to hate both Him and the rest of the family.

Of course not all Jesus' childhood miracles listed in the pseudo gospels are like these. He raises the dead, heals His brother James from the poison of a scorpion, lengthens a piece of wood for Joseph so that it fits after Joseph had cut it too short, etc. The Arabic Gospel of the Infancy abounds in such good works of Jesus performed when He was less than a year old. Pseudo Matthew also contains a mass of these imaginations.

But the Canonical Gospels of our familiar New Testament are for some reason totally free from all such extravagances. In these amazing writings there is not one vindictive miracle, not one useless display of supernatural power. Jesus never uses His extraordinary resource to comfort, convenience, or protect Himself. Instead He uses it to heal the sick, often making the spiritual significance of His physical cures explicit by a word. Once or twice He uses it to identify Himself with the glory of God, and with God's redemptive purpose. There is one instance in which He uses it as a parable of judgment—the withering of the fig tree, where the tree was made a symbol of Israel's hypocrisy.

Here, indeed, is a moral poise in the handling of the supernatural strikingly unique. It is something quite without parallel, either among the products of tradition, or even among the most expert creations of literary genius. Yet average men wrote the Gospels. Manifestly they could not have achieved such an amazing balance, except as the memory of an actual and incomparable historical figure had completely dominated their composition.

But the poise of the Canonical Gospels goes even a step further. They not only do not magnify the marvelous; but they entirely omit any description of it in the miracle records they do preserve. St. Matthew does, indeed, describe the gleaming countenance of the angel of the Resurrection, and his record does preserve that obscure item about the opening of Jerusalem's graves; but such matters are definitely unusual. Common enough in the pseudo gospels, a staple in such wonder writings as the *Lalita* of Buddhism, these fantastic accounts are wholly wanting in the New Testament.

The more you think about this contrast, the more you are bound to be astonished by it. The extravagances of the pseudographic gospels is about what you expect. They are about an average performance of the human mind when it attempts a description of the supernatural. So universal is this limitation upon man's powers that I do not remember ever to have read a satisfying imaginary treatment of the life of Jesus. But the Canonical Gospels manifest reserve, restraint, sobriety. Evidently some tremendous force had kept Christian imagination in check as long as the inner circle of Jesus' first followers remained in control. What was this force? I answer: It was an awe-inspiring sense of the majesty of that history with which they had come in contact, and with which they had been entrusted. They were men charged with the consummate self-manifestation of the living God, and they dared not change it. They were men who had lived with Jesus through three years, and then at the last had experienced both His cross and His resurrection. Men cannot experience such things without being lastingly affected by them.

The apostles and evangelists were thus affected; and it is this effect which we see in the constant contrasts between their records of Jesus and those of later writers who had not known their awe and responsibility.

IX

Myth or Mystery?

THE DISTINCTION BETWEEN MYTH AND HISTORY HAS
been constantly in the background in all that has
been said about the free use of imaginative material
by the writers of the pseudo-gospels. Now, however, this ultimate question must be squarely faced.

Adolf Harnack used to distinguish between what
he called the "Easter faith" and the "Easter fact."
The first he recognized as a true value. The second
he dismissed as unhistorical. This same distinction,
but without Harnack's language, is fairly common
in current criticism. Twice within a month I
have read discussions of the Resurrection by pro-
fessedly Christian theologians which take substantially Harnack's positions. They reject as unhistorical the New Testament details concerning
the Resurrection of Jesus; but they affirm the truth
of our Lord's triumph over death—one quite pas-
sionately, the other at least formally.

Lay believers will probably find themselves much
bewildered by what seems so evidently a contradictory position; but the explanation is simple. Uni-

versity circles are definitely slow to change major intellectual trends. Consequently it was to be expected that the momentum achieved by the naturalistic point of view during recent decades would still dominate even after the foundations of naturalism had been scientifically shattered. And this is precisely what has happened. Hostility to the supernatural is still shutting the doors of many minds against the historical Resurrection, notwithstanding the need of men's hearts for victory over death is so commanding that faith persists in spite even of the surrender of its facts.

Writers who take this position support it by two markedly different understandings. Some reduce the conviction of the apostles concerning their Master's triumph over death to a resultant of subjective forces. The memory of Jesus' goodness, the resurgence of their love for Him after the first terrific shock of the crucifixion, the moral necessity of His triumph in a theistic universe—such were the factors, they tell us, out of which the "Easter faith" was fashioned. Others, however, are sure there was some outward event which explains the apostolic conviction and exaltation. Jesus must have made Himself powerfully manifest to them, even though His resurrection, as history, cannot be admitted.

Facing these two positions, which, notwithstanding their marked differences, are yet equally negative toward the New Testament records of Jesus' risen appearances, I find myself wanting to say six things:

1. No limitation of reality, so as to exclude the supernatural (the transcendent), can be regarded as a conclusion of the natural sciences. The fact is this proposition cannot even be brought under the essential scientific tests.

2. But even if science could conclusively exclude the supernatural, radical criticism would not be accredited thereby, since criticism itself cannot be properly placed among the sciences. The natural sciences have achieved commanding recognition because they always have subjected their hypotheses and generalizations to objective tests. Criticism is not able to do this, and consequently it is not able to win for itself that recognition which universally men accord to the sciences.

The tests used by criticism in verifying its generalizations are most of the time subjective. Uusally they are limited to the measure of agreement an opinion is able to command among learned readers. But how remote such a consensus of opinion is from true scientific verification is manifest in the long history of critical mistakes. Prof. John Scott, formerly of Northwestern University, and himself a scholar of wide recognition, makes the statement that radical criticism has been uniformly wrong in its speculations. He adds that its irresponsibility has been proved again and again whenever archaeological facts have been discovered by which its speculations could be tested.[1]

3. Whether it be naturalistic speculation or criticism the refusal to admit the supernatural (the transcendent) within the bounds of possible reality is nothing but a choice in fundamental philosophy; and it is a negative choice, made in the face of the facts rather than as suggested by them.

The one force immediately known in experience is that of personal will—the individual's immediate sense of sovereignty, of mastership, with its accompanying feeling of moral responsibility. This basic experience is evidently more fundamental than man's developed awareness of the orderly mechanical forces about him which he catalogues as *nature*.

Consequently the proper conclusion would be to recognize nature as complex including at once *free, personal forces* and *standardized, mechanical*

[1] See Professor Scott's discussion of this matter in *We Would Know Jesus*, p. 90. However, he made this statement even stronger in a personal letter to the writer.

forces, or else to seek unity by explaining the less immediately known *mechanical forces* in terms of the more immediately known *personal forces*. Either one of these procedures would leave abundant room for the biblical supernaturals, including that of the historical Resurrection. The third course, the one actually taken by all naturalistic speculations, and presupposed by all radical criticism, seeks to explain the ultimate experience of *free personal force* in terms of the derived experience of *standardized, mechanical force*. Such a procedure, as I have said, cannot be understood otherwise than as a negative choice in fundamental philosophy, and a choice made in opposition to facts rather than as suggested by them.

4. But, as the scientist might say, let us by hypothesis suppose the Resurrection of Jesus to have been an historical fact, and precisely such a fact as the New Testament describes—how then could a man, who might have chosen to maintain the naturalistic front to the universe, come in contact with it? Answer: For such an one there is no possibility of making contact. His chosen limitations upon reality shut him away from every possible contact with anything which transcends those limitations. The conclusion is unescapable: *No matter how majestic such a man's intellect, or how*

*broad his learning, his chosen point of view inca-
pacitates him from making an evaluation of the
New Testament witness to Jesus.*

5. But regardless of any prejudice against the
supernatural, man's myth-making tendency itself
bears powerful witness to the tragic inadequacy
of life's limiting natural. Evidently man is too big
for the universe which houses him; and so he experiences a perpetual urge to seek escape from it.
His myth-making tendency is just one manifestation
of this urge. But man's myth-making tendency,
which presses him to seek escape from the limitations of nature, is itself a part of nature. Nature
thus includes within itself a prophetic voice fore-
announcing some such transcendent invasion of its
inadequate order as the resurrection of Jesus Christ
from the dead. The supernatural is thus necessary
to the fulfillment of the natural, for aspiration is as
much a part of the universe as energy or entropy.

6. There is one concluding criticism of the na-
uralistic prejudice; and here every negative speculation concerning the Resurrection breaks down
decisively. It is a matter quite beyond dispute
that some tremendous circumstance did take place
back there in Jerusalem in the year A.D. 30; and this
event, whatever it may have been, did fill men
and women with a conquering conviction of Jesus'

historic victory over death. This conviction not only enabled those people to despise death, but it also enabled them to transform history.

Intermittently through nine generations, and at times quite consecutively, those men and women endured persecution. The fact is persecutions assailed them even before the Christian movement was well established. It is impossible to say just how soon, but certainly within a year or so after St. Peter preached that first Christian sermon on the day of Pentecost, believers were compelled to flee the Holy City. But this difficult experience did not dim their conviction or quench their enthusiasm. Driven from Jerusalem, they found in their adversity only a goad to compel their wider proclamation of the glorious gospel of Christ's victory over death, and of His all-sufficient Saviourhood.

Here evidently, then, was a force with the sweep and power of an earthquake. And like an earthquake it struck the apostolic group. Immediately everything was changed. When Criticism says this force was just a psychological resultant, I answer: Those who so explain the apostles do not themselves have a tithe of the power which surged in that primitive Christian community. Let me put it this way: *The Apostolic shout of the Resurrection made Christians of the first century worship Jesus*

*with joy, even when that worship meant martyrdom.
Our psychological substitute for their victory shout
has so diminished the modern Christian's regard for
Jesus, that many of us are indifferent to His worship, notwithstanding it is not only safe, but even
comfortable.*

One cannot face this contrast in attitudes without realizing, both that there was more behind the
original Christian witness to the Resurrection than
a mere psychological reaction, and also that the
modern Church has been wrong in making terms
with the contemporary naturalistic prejudice. The
power of appeal of the Christian Gospel is precisely
the confirmation—the reinforcement—its mighty
facts bring to the longings of man's soul. It is
when objective history has been added to subjective
longing, that sublimity develops an effective authority, and men even dare the mist-enshrouded
heights. The tale of the Christian centuries is
chiefly the story of just such adventuring. The
soaring aspiration of men's souls, being reinforced
by the record of Christ's glory in history, they have
adventured, and adventuring, they have experienced.

Consequently, I hold it to be a conclusion of
history that the Easter faith and the Easter fact
cannot be separated; that the Resurrection is not

myth but history; and that in the clear recognition of this glorious truth is the enduring power of the Church.

More and more I am coming to see not only life, but truth as a choice; and usually the choice is between two antipodal possibilities. Such, in fact, is the circumstance now confronting modern men: We can recognize free force (the supernatural), or we can surrender to futility and despair. Thus two groups of men and two general viewpoints are being stood in juxtaposition—the one over against the other. On the one hand we see St. Peter, St. John, and St. Paul, with their confidence in the historic supernatural and all its promise. On the other hand we see such negative thinkers as Lord Bertrand Russell, Sir Arthur Keith, Aldous Huxley,[2] etc., with their "unyielding despair," and their "futilitarianism." Between are the multitude of men and women who have not yet either fully found or fully lost themselves, but who are ever being confronted by the ageless witness of the Christian Church.

Yes, it is indeed as James Orr so powerfully said more than a quarter of a century ago: There is no stopping place for the human mind between the

[2] Huxley has now given up his Naturalism and his "Futilitarianism," having returned to faith.

glory of a complete faith in Christ, and the bottom-less abyss of pessimism and despair.[3] If Jesus be myth, then life is hopeless, and truth is vanity and illusion. But if Jesus be history, if the New Testament portrait of Him be, by and large, a responsible statement of actual facts, then He is just one more glorious mystery which has been made manifest in the evolutionary increase of the cosmos. The original Divine volitioning of light is a mystery; why then should the later Divine revelation of Eternal Life be rejected because it is a mystery? The fact is, there are many mysteries. Enumerate some of them—light, life, consciousness, personality, Revelation, Incarnation, Resurrection. Naturalism demands that we eliminate the last three—but why? I answer: There is no reason except the negative choice of certain thinkers toward the transcendent. These men are so determined to have a little mechanical universe that they refuse all evidence tending to establish a nobler one.

[3] Compare the main drive of Professor Orr's thinking in his *Christian View of God and the World.*

X

The Risen Christ Related to the Universe

"THINK DEEPLY OR BE DAMNED"—THIS ABOUT PUTS the conclusion to which we came in the last chapter; and while this principle cannot be applied to all individuals, it can and must be applied to all social groups.

There is indeed a level of thinking and living which moves on to inevitable increase; and there is a level of thinking and living which cannot make advance, but must decline. That moral and spiritual upheaval we know as the Protestant Reformation was first of all an intellectual movement. It changed the average man from one who merely looked at pictures to one who read and thought. A resulting new average of spirituality was to be expected, and it was realized. American democracy was a political resultant of this. America was the achievement of a population whose basic concern had become spiritual. Our American fathers were men who believed high things. They read and thought upon high things; and the consequence was, they achieved the sublime liberties and progress of this civilization.

The general decline of democracy today is of course due to our reduced spirituality. Too many of us modern men neither believe the great nobilities, nor yet read and think about them. For two generations, we have been increasingly preoccupied with things; we have neglected the spirit: and both our crime wave and the decline of democracy are the consequences. These results were as inevitable as the certainty that an uncultivated garden will become a place of disorder, choked with weeds.

The call to deep and high thinking involved in all this cannot be missed. It is here, and here alone free men will find the answer to encroachments by totalitarian tyrannies. We modern men must learn once more to think deeply, that is to think in terms of philosophy: for science is, by its very principles, less than fundamental in its approach to reality.

But the new science itself is now pointing us to philosophy. It is now affirming that the ultimate ground of objective things is spirit. Matter, these leaders say, is not *stuff:* it is force; it is a complex of interacting forces; and these forces seem to resolve into mental values—into the "mathematical formulae" of Jeans—into ideas of an Infinite Mind.

Consequently the place for modern men to begin,

when they would seek to comprehend the resurrection of Jesus Christ from the dead, is with infinite mind, with the Infinite Consciousness. Starting so, the objective universe becomes just a complex conception continuously conceived within His awareness.

On this basis we must conceive of God as forever thinking and willing every single proton and electron which is included within the total mass of the universe. These forces must be seen as ceaselessly flowing from His imagination and will, much as the rays of light do from the moving-picture projector. The basic force of the universe would thus be the free, the personal will of God; and the uniformity of nature, which we have identified as *natural law*, would become just a standardization in the expression of God's free purposings.

Starting thus, with personality, we discover that our orderly universe is not a necessity, but a choice. God could have willed a fairy world of fantastic confusion. In point of fact, He did not will such a world, and for two reasons: A world of confusion and disorder would not have expressed the orderliness of His own holy life. A fairy world, in which there was no fixed natural order, would not have been a fit home for those free moral personalities with which He purposed to crown creation.

And so because God willed, and still does will it, we have this orderly universe. It expresses, but it does not limit Him. He respects it, but it does not confine Him. To hold otherwise than this is to replace one's theism with pantheism or atheism, denying God.

Science tells us that for æons God's universe was just a lifeless mechanical order. Its evolution involved the continuous running down of atomic energy. They call it "katagenesis." Then in a fullness of time God willed life. It was a local running-up process, opposed to katagenesis, and known as "anagenesis." This new anagenetic force was at last overcome by the katagenetic trend, and life was overwhelmed in death.

Then once again there were æons, until a second time God willed a new creative purpose. He stood moral personality at the summit of life and of creation. And quite regardless of any evolutionary facts or speculations, the appearance of man involves a new Divine creative purpose, for man is more than protons and electrons. Man is consciousness, self-consciousness, moral self-consciousness, like God's own eternal being. In creating finite personality God has given of His own very nature to man. He has, if we may use the figure, willed new centers of finite consciousness within the sweep of His infinite awareness. St. Paul was not speaking in figures of speech, but most literally, when he said, "In Him we live, and move, and have our being."

And now, having achieved a fairly clear outline of a Christian world view, we are in position to answer two questions of basic significance for our whole study of Jesus' resurrection. These questions are:

a. In a universe which is spiritual in its ground— in a universe which is in fact an imagination willed into reality within the infinite consciousness of God —how shall we understand natural law?

b. In a universe whose every force continuously flows from the free creative will of God, how shall we conceive the supernatural—the miraculous?

The answer to the first of these questions is instant. If the universe is something perpetually formed within the infinite consciousness of the living God by His free imagination and will, then natural law must be a mere standardization of this His free activity. The regularity of the universe is thus not something of necessity, but instead, it merely reflects the sovereign purpose of God the Father Almighty.

The answer to the second question is also and equally definite. In a universe in which all action is fundamentally personal will, the supernatural can differ from the natural only in being a new act apart from, and independent of, the whole. A miracle would thus be any new creative act of God. It might be the creation of life in the midst of a mechanistic universe, or the creation of moral personality in the midst of an animal universe, or the revelation of Eternal Life in the midst of a dying universe. Or it might be something less cosmically significant—a revelation given to some finite intellect such as Charles G. Finney or Joan of Arc.

The important thing for the Christian is to see that the supernatural—the free—the new expression of God's imagination and will—is something to be expected in a personalistic universe. Belief in the supernatural is thus just belief in the free self-expression of personality; and its reality is essential at once to the integrity of personal God, to the integrity and dignity of personal man, and to the reality of religion.

As thus conceived, Jesus' resurrection is no more a violation of nature than a mother's extraordinary expression of her love is a violation of the ordinary morality of her faithful devotion. In each case we simply have a free personality doing a new thing. The trouble with the naturalistic speculation, when built upon the basis of theism, is, the two are inconsistent. They are like a man's head on a horse's body. Naturalism excludes personality; and the affirmation of personality excludes naturalism (more exactly, it limits the natural to a limited standardization of God's free purposing).

But, asks some one, precisely what did happen in that august cosmic moment of the first Easter Day? And here, indeed, is a question worthy of the best wisdom of the human race! There is, however, no answer, for none but God can plumb the mystery of His power. Remember, the protons and electrons, of which the mortal body of the Son of God was constituted, were not solid things. They were but so many individual ideas—"mathematical formulæ," and no more. God thought them, and willed them into reality within His consciousness. They were real for Him, and for every other finite center of self-consciousness whom He had willed within His infinitude. They, indeed, resemble in one respect the rays of light which stream from the moving picture projector. These rays have no identity and no continuity. The only identity and continuity in connection with them concerns the pattern they form upon the screen.

Think now with vivid philosophical realism. All night Friday and through that tremendous Sabbath Day the Infinite Mind and Will must have been creating and recreating the mortal body of His Son as it rested there upon its stone couch in Joseph's tomb. Then came Easter morning; and the Divine willing was changed. The pattern remained the same, but the nature of the forces which had been constituting it were radically altered. They were metamorphosed into something different—something they never had been before. By this metamorphosis Jesus' body of death became a new body of glory. It became the perfect instrument of His now triumphant spirit.

It is idle to ask, How? Neither our science, nor yet our philosophy, can answer any ultimate *how*. But our science does give us significant help. Our fathers used to know substance under three forms. They knew it as a solid in ice. They heated the ice and metamorphosed it into water. They boiled the water and metamorphosed it into steam. A few scant years ago this was our limit; but today we go far beyond that limit. Now we bombard the atoms of this water or ice with some powerful ray, knocking out of them protons and electrons, or perhaps exploding them into their constituent factors. And what are these factors? Poincare answers: They are pulsations in empty space (he does not any longer even assume the theoretical ether).

Rigid ice—flowing water—an invisible illusive gas —a vastly more illusive thing, some pulsation, some interacting concentration of pulsations—this is matter as the newest science describes it. Confronting such varied manifestations, and such ultimately illusive values, it does not seem too difficult to conceive that the God, from whose creative will it all forever flows, could transform it into yet another form. Nor does it seem too difficult to conceive that this final form might be one in which it would be the perfect servant of all glorified spirits, beginning with that of His Son, whom redemptively He raised from the dead.

Of course there is a leap of faith here; but even if our best scientists could have been back there at Joseph's sepulcher with their chemistry and their microscopes, they would not have been able even so to have intercepted the mystery of Easter's majestic metamorphosis. They could no more have intercepted it than they can right now intercept the mystery in the multiplied metamorphoses which are taking place beneath their very eyes every time inorganic matter is transformed into living protoplasm. These contemporary metamorphoses do not, indeed, seem to us mysterious because they happen so often, and so have become familiar: whereas the historic metamorphosis which took place in the tomb of Joseph of Arimathaea, being unfamiliar, startles us into unbelief. The attitude is, of course, definitely superficial and confused. Neither familiarity nor unfamiliarity has anything to do with the nature of mystery. Thus the passing of time is the most familiar of experiences; and yet it is also completely mysterious. If it were not for the fact that men do so constantly experience time, reason would have disproved it centuries ago. Mystery has, thus, nothing to do with the familiarity of an experience, or its unfamiliarity. All mystery is simply an immediate experience of fundamental reality. If any experience be a true mystery, it will remain a mystery always. It is like the intuitions, which are seen as true, but can never be explained. It is like what Professor Brightman calls the "brute facts." All you can do with any mystery is experience it, and rejoice in it.

These things being true, the stumbling of modern men at the mystery of the Resurrection is most unimpressive intellectually. Instead of assuming that the values of physical and animal nature bounded reality, and then asking whether the Resurrection be credible, they should have faced the mystery of

the Resurrection by asking, whether there were
any other mysteries, or facts, which suggested and
demanded it? Had they asked this latter question,
they would have confronted immediately:

The mystery of man's immense aspirational life;

The mystery of man's sense of duty and righteousness, with its deep dependence upon his whole
aspirational life;

The fact that faith in the Resurrection demonstrably enlarges man's creativity, and every capacity of his life;

The fact that the whole evolutionary movement
of the ages had stopped short with man; and that
the universe was thus definitely without either the
fulfillment of its potentialities, or a worthy goal,
until this new mystery energized it to a new advance.

It is within this majestic setting that the sincere
thinker is obliged to place the New Testament
witness to the mystery of Jesus' victory over death;
and in doing so he can have this confidence: *That
there is no philosophy, and no science which either
does, or can, exclude the revelation of that great
new mystery.* The Christian is entitled to go a
step farther. He can remind himself and other
men that the Christian records were written by men
with joy—yes, with joy, notwithstanding the ig-

nominy and death which were heaped upon them because of their testimony: and he can bear witness to this modern world that if it will believe, it also will experience the joy which made those other men more than conquerors in their day.

XI

With What Body?

HOLDING DEFINITELY IN MIND THE ULTIMATELY
spiritual nature of physical things, which both
science and philosophy now suggest, we are at
last in position to turn to the New Testament, and
to investigate the character of the resurrection body
of Jesus. The best procedure will be at first to attempt no harmonization, but simply to set down
all the significant facts.

And of these the primary one is evidently the
identity between the mortal body of Jesus which
was buried, and the glorified body which was raised
from the dead. The New Testament records are all
explicit at this point. The type of Resurrection
which took place that first Easter morning was
one which left the tomb of Jesus empty behind it.

The Resurrection accounts in all four of the
evangelists begin with the open, empty sepulcher.
The three synoptic records follow immediately with
an angelic message, affirming the Risen Lord and
pointing to the empty couch where His mortal
body had rested. The Fourth Gospel adds the

interesting item of the early morning visit of St. Peter and St. John to the sepulcher, and their examination of the graveclothes which they found. The charge of the Jews, that the disciples had stolen the Master's body, made any apolgetic use of the empty tomb impossible. Consequently this circumstance was not emphasized in primitive Christian preaching. The empty sepulcher was, however, and from the very beginning, a part of the tradition.

The careful observer will be interested to notice the inclusion of this detail in St. Luke and St. Matthew as well as in St. Mark and St. John: for while both of the two latter reflect the recollections of eyewitnesses, the two former do not. St. Luke represents an historical investigation made in the year 57, and St. Matthew embodies the general tradition as current, say about the year 70.

But though the identity of Jesus' body of death with the body of His resurrection is steadily assumed, a marked difference is noted in it. St. Luke says specifically that the Risen Jesus "vanished." The Greek is most vivid; it runs, "But their eyes were opened and they knew Him; and He became invisibly away from them." In English it would be, "He vanished into invisibility away from them." [1]

[1] Compare St. Luke 24:31, Vincent's *Word Studies, ad loc.*

not meant to diminish the glory of the vision, but only the worthiness of the recipient. The other apostles came to their experience of the Risen Christ out of years of earlier intimacy with Him. They had some equipment for their apostleship; but St. Paul saw himself as far different. As compared with them, he saw himself as no more than an abortion.

In evaluating St. Paul's identification of his own experience of the Risen Christ along with those given to the other apostles, it is important to notice that St. Paul's own experience is described as fully objective. Not only St. Paul, but the soldiers, saw the blinding light. It is probable also that the soldiers heard some sound, notwithstanding they did not comprehend the Hebrew words spoken. The triple record of St. Paul's conversion, preserved in The Acts, is not explicit upon this last item; but, after careful comparison, I am inclined to think the soldiers also heard some sound. However, the clear objectivity of the great light alone would establish the cosmic character of the experience. The Risen Christ evidently was made manifest from heaven.[6]

The nature of all objective experience is so utter-

[6] Compare I Corinthians 15:3-8, and Acts 9:1-9; 22:6-12; 26:12-19.

ly mysterious that one feels much hesitation in attempting any synthesis of the New Testament data.

In addition to those pre-ascension manifestations of the Risen Christ, and the later blinding manifestation given to St. Paul, the New Testament preserves also the record of a vision granted to the dying Stephen (The Acts 7:56), as well as a later one given to St. Paul. Beside these, there were doubtless other such experiences during apostolic times; and Christian biography records not a few in the centuries between then and now. How shall we think of these phenomena? To dismiss them instantly as hallucinations is far from scientific; and since Professor Rhine's discovery of the unity of all consciousness [7] it will be found very far from satisfying.

Take the deathbed visions of Jesus so often given to believers; take that remarkable vision vouchsafed to Charles G. Finney, which issued in a gospel ministry almost apostolic in its attending spiritual phenomena—how shall we explain these? Personally I am satisfied that all such experiences do have what I will call *an objective cause*—that is, they are produced by some immediate dealing with the be-

[7] Professor Rhine, in his *New Frontiers of the Mind*, definitely affirms the reality of perceptions not grounded in any sense experience, but dependent upon the unmediated impact of mind upon mind.

liever upon the part of the glorified Christ. Suppose we use Dr. Finney's experience as the norm of all post-apostolic experiences. Here is his own description of it:

He had gone to the woods to pour out his soul in prayer, having been for some time under a terrific burden of sin. As he made his way into a place screened by heavy foliage he said within himself, "I will give my heart to God, or I will never come down." He arrived; he dropped upon his knees; he began to pray. And then suddenly he discovered that he could not pray. His mind seemed divided between a desire to make contact with God, and a fear that someone would see him. Every rustling of the leaves caused him to open his eyes to see if he were being observed. This divided attitude of his heart shocked and disgusted him. He saw his deep sinfulness; he saw his enormous pride: and in self-despair he at last broke down before God.

At that moment of complete self-abandon a Scripture seemed to drop into his mind. It ran, "Then shall ye go and pray unto me, and I will harken unto you. Then shall ye seek and find me, when ye shall search for me with a whole heart." Though he could not remember having read the words, he nevertheless identified them as Scripture; and cast himself upon the grace of God with a unity of purpose that made him as certain of his Godward trust as he was of his existence. Following this believing venture upon his part many passages of Scripture flooded his consciousness. They seemed, as he said, not so much to fall into his intellect as into his heart; and he laid hold upon them with abandon of a drowning man.

Finney had spent nearly the whole of the morning there in the woods communing with God; and as at last he made his way from his leafy sanctuary he was conscious that his mind "had become wonderfully quiet and peaceful." It was noon on the 10th of October, 1821. He went to dinner; but he could not eat. He went to his law office, and taking his bass-viol began to sing Christian hymns; but he could not sing for weeping. He spent the afternoon helping the squire, his employer, move his law library and office furniture to new quarters: and during all those hours of physical work he was conscious of a great depth of peace, and of an eagerness to be alone in prayer.

Just at dark the squire went home. Finney accompanied him to the door; and said good night. He shut it, and was alone. Instantly his heart was "liquid within" him. He rushed into the back office where there was neither fire nor light, to pour out his soul in prayer. He closed the inner door behind him, and noticed that the room seemed illuminated, and that the Lord Jesus Christ was there. He met Him "face to face." Writing of that experience, he records: "It did not occur to me then, nor did it for some time afterwards, that it was wholly a mental state. On the contrary, it seemed to me that I saw Him as I would see any other man. . . . . I fell down at His feet and poured out my soul to Him. I wept aloud like a child, and made such confessions as I could with my choked utterance. It seemed to me that I bathed His feet with my tears; and yet I had no distinct impression that I touched Him that I recollect."

How long this experience continued Finney did not know; but he had made a large fire in the front office just before he went into the back room, and when he returned it had nearly burned out. He started to sit down by the fire, his heart full of wonder because of the experience he had just passed through, when another came upon him. A sensation as of waves of electricity, one following another, seemed to pass through his being. And yet these waves were not quite like electricity, for they were not so purely physical. They were rich with a sense of love. "It seemed like the very breath of

God. I can recollect distinctly that it seemed to fan me, like immense wings." [8]

Directly after this experience Mr. Finney gave up the practice of law. He took up the work of a Christian witness, and then, almost immediately, of an evangelist. The striking circumstance was that everywhere Mr. Finney went there were at once extraordinary religious phenomena, with deep conviction of sin. The village of Adams, in Oneida County, New York, became a radiant center of spiritual power.

I want now to stand over against each other these four sets of facts:

First, the Resurrection manifestations of Jesus between Easter and Ascension. These involve three things: (a) The metamorphosis of the Saviour's mortal body placed in the sepulcher on Good Friday evening. (b) The production of a body which was at once tangible, and yet also transcendent to the limitations of space and substance as we are familiar with them. (c) The production of a body in expressive identity with all that the Son of God had been as an historic figure. Both the empty sepulcher and the circumstance that these manifesta-

---

[8] *Memories of the Rev. Charles G. Finney*, pp. 14-21, abbreviated. The record bears the date 1876. The book is a Fleming H. Revell publication.

difficulty, for the powers of the mind, even in
nature, vary widely. Some men can see twice as
far as others. A Beethoven can hear music in his
mind. A Shakespeare can turn words into music.
A Darwin can be so preoccupied with logical
generalizations that he loses his capacity to appreciate. The analytical intellect can live in a world
the practical mind can scarcely enter. The mind
attuned to supersensory impressions can discern
unexpressed thoughts. Mental capacities, then,
vary within nature; and there is no reason at all to
assume that nature exhausts them. Unquestionably
Eternal Life will disclose new powers; and if God
in His wisdom lends some of these to chosen instru-
ments—prophets and apostles, etc.—there is no reason why reason should be scandalized. Such a
supposition is necessary to any understanding of the
New Testament data: for Jesus' resurrection com-
bines historical values, like the metamorphosis of
His body of death to produce an empty tomb, with
superhistorical values, like His glorified manifestations to chosen witnesses. The confusion is unavoidable, for two worlds were meeting; and two
worlds had to meet. The heavenly world, which
man knows only in his aspirations, was stooping
to touch earth's failing world of mere physical and

rational resource. It was one of God's supreme "fullnesses of time."

Gathering up at this point, our conclusion would be, that however we may try to conceive the nature of the Saviour's risen body, we are forced to admit that the whole apostolic company, including St. Paul, did come in contact with what seemed to them an objectively manifest person. Nor should we be too sure that the same was not the case with St. Stephen, and with others down the Christian centuries. At the first, Dr. Finney so regarded his own experience. Later, as he thought about it, he was inclined to regard it as merely subjective. From our point of view, since no one else shared his vision, we find ourselves unable to apply to it any test for objectivity. However, to reject such a possibility because it would involve the glorified body of the risen Saviour in a frequent shuttling back and forth between earth and heaven, is hardly legitimate. Both the glorified body of the Saviour and heaven itself are evidently transcendent to the limitations of our cosmic space. The fact is we are beyond ourselves when we attempt to apply either our imagination or our halting reason to the circumstances of the Infinite.

It is indeed as St. Paul said: The Christian's life is a mystery hidden in the wisdom and resource of

God. And it is this very mysterious character of
it which causes our self-sufficient lives to hesitate
and stumble at it. Both Jesus and His resurrection,
and the gospel which rises in Him, belong to a
higher plane of experience than that at which we
are accustomed to live. We greatly need that
higher plane; nevertheless we do sometimes both
fear and resent it. We resent it because it humbles
us in our self-sufficiency. We fear it because it re-
proves our sins. Then, too, that plane of thinking is
difficult for us, because most of the time we do not
think deeply. Instead, we just classify our experiences by comparing them with familiar patterns;
and we mistake familiarity for comprehension.
Thus, we locate an event in springtime, or autumn;
and are quite unconscious of the mystery of time.
Or we purchase a pair of glasses, which improve
our sight, and suppose the science of optics has
explained the mystery of seeing. All this is of
course dreadfully on the surface; and modern thinking has been tragically superficial. The fact is,
one of our deep needs is just that we come to recognize this fact, and that we dare to undertake something more basic. St. Paul projected a bit of tremendous thinking into one of his sermons. He
said that men live and move and have their being
in God; and if we could attain to the meaning

locked up in these words, we would have achieved a world view large enough for science, for religion, and for the resurrection of Jesus Christ.

Dare we undertake it? Conceive, then, one Infinite Consciousness, within which we, ourselves, are finite centers, willed into existence by the creative purpose of God the Father Almighty. The universe also is a structure willed within the inclusiveness of this Infinite Consciousness. And now, since all creation, both worlds, life, and personalities, are either willed images or willed centers within the Infinite Awareness, it is possible to understand how we can both see and feel and hear. I can know that which God thinks and wills, because I am one consciousness with Him. His is the Infinite Consciousness which comprehends the whole in one vast inclusiveness. Mine is a finite center of awareness which He has willed within Himself. The whole of His plentitude is indeed available for me, but it will take eternity for me to explore it.

Within the structure of this world view every fact of science and every fact of revelation can find its proper place; and the resurrection of Jesus Christ from the dead becomes almost a necessary factor within the whole great scheme. The specific nature of the resurrection body will, indeed, still remain a mystery; but it will be no more a mystery than the specific nature of our own present physical bodies. There is this single difference between the two mysteries: The first is an unfamiliar mystery. The second is a familiar mystery.

Christ's resurrection body and our own earth bodies are after all only patterns—complex ideas willed into reality within the consciousness of the Infinite: and, consequently, the metamorphosis of one pattern into another is no more a problem for God than those simple changes which an artist often makes in the structure of his compositions. Our whole modern mistake has been just the old one of a self-sufficient mood, and of a superficial view.

We have wanted to feel our intellects adequate to the mystery of life; so we have accepted space and time, matter, force, and personal consciousness, assuming that we did comprehend them. Then, even worse, we have standardized our inadequate outlook as being the true boundary of reality—we have denied everything else, saying it could not be. So we have created our blighting scientific naturalism, materialism, futilitarianism, atheism; and confined life within a dungeon of our own making. Despairing of any real goal for life, we have built the hypocrisies of our Communism, our Naziism, our humanistic utopianism; and then came 1940, and the collapse of our silly dreams.

XII

His Cosmic Significance

ALREADY WE HAVE NOTED THAT JESUS DIVIDES history; that quite apart from the formality of chronology, all time before Him is necessarily B.C., and all time after Him A.D. This fact will be admitted on every hand. It is something unescapable; but what is its explanation?

Many will answer by referring to Jesus' truth, and to His teaching ministry. This explanation, however, is quite inadequate: for great as was Jesus' truth, His teaching ministry was so brief, and so irregularly developed, that it would be absurd to regard it the explanation of His supreme position in history.

Indeed, truth alone is quite inadequate as the explanation of the Christian movement, and for several reasons. In the first place the masses of men have never explored the basic essentials of Jesus' philosophy of life, and they do not now know them. Jesus' basic truth was sonship—an uninterrupted dependence upon the guidance of His Father. The contemporary humanistic benevolence, which passes for it is as remote from the actual insight of Jesus as was that Phariseeism, which He denounced so vigorously.

Then in the second place, the failure of life is deeper than its ignorance of the ideal. Greek philosophers, themselves, while teaching salvation by truth, nevertheless, limited it to the few. They had no idea that men generally could be saved by truth. The Greeks of course were doubly wrong. They were wrong in their philosophy of salvation, and in their limitation of it to the few. The evil, however, from which men must be saved is deeper than ignorance; it is nothing less that a corrupting viewpoint and motive of self-centeredness for which there is no other cure than the grace and omnipotence of God.

Then yet once more, both salvation and the historical supremacy of Jesus require that He should be the object of men's powerful affections; and His brief teaching ministry of two thousand years ago, or this, even with the addition of his noble example, cannot explain man's enduring love for Him. Evidently, then, there is another factor. Jesus, the teacher, can explain neither the Christian movement nor his own commanding position in history.

But now, I can hear some one saying, "Correct! Something else is necessary beside Jesus' teaching ministry; and that something else is, of course, His martyrdom. It is the Jesus whose teaching and living became His cross who occupies the central position in history; and who has transformed through men's love of Him all the centuries since His day."

This opinion, however, no more than the previous one, will stand the test of history. The fact is, the record of the centuries is fairly rich in the high devotion of martyrdom; and yet no one of the martyrs, with the exception of Jesus, has attained to the supreme position in history.

Indeed, one could go a step farther. The fact is mere martyrdom does not demonstrate either sincerity or devotion. During the French revolution it was the exception when men lacked the courage to die nobly; and yet their motives were as frequently mere sporting pride, as they were principle.

But not to dismiss too swiftly the creative value of martyrdom as an explanation of Jesus' unique position in history, let us compare Him with Socrates. The Athenian teacher unquestionably died for principle. He was a martyr in every sense in which the word can be applied to Jesus. Furthermore Plato and Xenophon loved him with as sincere a human devotion as St. Mark and St. John did

Jesus. Yes, from the point of view of strictly naturalistic opportunities, Plato, and Xenophon had
a better chance to make Socrates a universal figure,
than St. Peter and St. John had to do the same for
the crucified Jesus. Yet Plato and Xenophon failed,
and St. Peter and St. John succeeded. What is the
difference?

Athens, where the martyrdom of Socrates took
place, was the intellectual center of the ancient
world, Jerusalem, where Jesus was crucified, was,
by comparison, a provincial Jewish community.
Plato and Xenophon were ranking men of letters
in their notable world. The original apostolic company included not one man of literary ability or of
learned recognition. Humanly speaking, the probabilities were all definitely against the success of the
followers of Jesus, and definitely favorable to the
friends of Socrates. Nevertheless, in spite of probabilities and improbabilities, the followers of Jesus
did make His the one universal name in history;
whereas the friends of Socrates failed so completely
to do this, that few men know much about him,
and multitudes do not even know the century in
which he lived.

What is the explanation of this amazing difference?

I answer instantly: The final record about Soc-

rates was that of the tragedy and pathos of a defeat.
Mere sentimentalities put aside, death is grim defeat;
and the final record about Socrates was that he died.
But the final record about Jesus is different. Beyond that entombment in a borrowed grave by two
timid friends while weeping women watched from
afar, there is another chapter. It begins with an
earthquake—then an empty tomb—then a vision of
angels. After these, come the manifestations of
Jesus Himself. He is magnificent in victory He
asserts all authority. "Go ye," he says, "disciple
all nations . . . . and, lo, I am with you always, even
unto the end of the ages."

And it seems that this final chapter, so begun,
simply cannot have an end. Again and again His
movement has been beset with terrific opposition;
but always it has burst through, becoming ever
more powerful. There is, indeed, something endless
about Jesus; and this inherent endlessness of His
impact is the climatic proof of His living reality.
The fact is, the resurrection of Jesus is at once a
cosmic and an historical necessity. It is a cosmic
necessity, because without it there is no completeness for man, either as an individual, or as a society.
It is an historical necessity, because without it there
is no explanation of that evident forward surge
in history which makes the recent centuries such a

striking contrast to all the piled-up millenniums before. Remember, it was not until the Reformation
that a firmly established Christian world view was
at last given to the intelligence of a whole continent.
But now in less than half a millennium the results
of that achievement are manifest in an almost
world-wide development of freedom, science, civilization. Do you doubt the relationship between
these values? Then stop to consider how swiftly
progress has been halted and free civilization under-
mined, since the truth of Christ's transcendent person has been widely called in question.

Here is a picture with that characteristic con-
clusiveness which breadth of outlook can give. As
Asiatic civilization had died, so European civilization was dying from Aristotle forward. Following
Aristotle the blight of skepticism descended upon
that world; and with skepticism came inevitable
despair. But the rise of despair is the beginning of
death for any civilization. Despairing men are
never creative. And so European culture was dying, when about 6 B.C. Jesus, Messiah, was born of
Mary in a grotto in the hills of Bethlehem.

That obscure event changed everything. It was
but a Jewish incident; but it burst all its boundaries
and became universal. The life, teaching, death,
and resurrection of this peasant boy did something

to a dying age. It changed the point of view from which men looked out upon life. It transformed and energized their motives. It created new customs, new standards, new institutions, and a new philosophy. In a word, His personal Resurrection produced the resurrection of a civilization. Europe came back to life.

But the world today has been experiencing once again something of the same inhibiting skepticism and despair which followed Aristotle. The blight of our naturalistic speculations has made our universe too small for us. Having abolished everything but mechanical forces—matter and energy—we have been under the necessity of satisfying our unbounded aspirations with a mere abundance of things. It is because of this inadequacy in our outlook that we have conceived the absurdity of our economic heavens—our this-world utopias, built out of self-centered men, enriched with an abundance of things.

A word further here. The misconception of Karl Marx was that he built his final goal upon the humanly self-sufficient philosophy of Hegel, rather than upon the sonship philosophy of Jesus. Consequently starting with self-sufficient, self-centered men and women, he had to approach unity through conflict, and brotherhood through satiety of desire.

The dictatorship of the proletariat was to become an inclusive brotherhood when satiety had so extinguished desire as to make conflict any longer meaningless.

Doubtless Marx was a man of broad learning, who did make a notable contribution to economic thought. However, his whole conception is shockingly out of contact with reality.

There is no way out of man's deep self-centeredness into sonship, brotherhood, and social unity except the one Jesus proclaimed—the way of dying unto self, and of being made alive again by the inner revelation of another and different viewpoint. Marx's class conflict is evil and futility; and it never can bring the race into its destiny. The accomplishments of Jesus' program, of losing one's self to find one's self, fill the pages of history. The tragedy of modern times is that, motivated by the same rationalistic self-sufficiency as that which motivated Marx, modern men, widely, have turned their backs upon Jesus, and learned instead the dark absurdity of class conflict.

How silly, yes, sinful, we have been! The self-sufficient viewpoint never did and never will get the human race anywhere. The decay of Greek culture, more than two millenniums ago, proves that man left to himself cannot arrive at truth. And the collapse of Greek freedom, at the same time, proves that man left to his own resources cannot maintain free institutions. Three conclusions stand forth with clarity:

a. The deep failure of the human race is precisely its absurd love of self-sufficiency, self-exaltation, etc. In life terms this viewpoint is the poverty of secularism. In intellectual terms it is the absurdity of naturalism. And wherever secularism and naturalism become dominant, there is, first, social decay, and then, tyranny, as a necessary defense against anarchy.

b. The human race has tried this self-sufficient, self-centered, front to life during piled-up millenniums. The story of its accomplishments has been that of failures repeating themselves with the monotony of a refrain. Only in the Bible do we have the basis for a philosophy of history; and only in Jesus Christ do we have the forces requisite to a significant historical increase.

c. Man cannot attain to that destiny of which intuitively he is aware, except in conscious dependence upon God. Our race's absolute necessity is for a Divine supernatural resource which is at once revealing and creative. The crowning truth of the cosmos is thus not the mechanically ordered relations of the stars, unified by gravitation; but instead the free fellowship of personalities, unified by moral love. So above the mechanical must be the free, and above the natural must be the supernatural. And man's salvation is essentially in reaching beyond himself and his natural universe to lay hold upon the freely acting God—the God who came near to us in the Incarnation in order that He might woo us to Himself.

The supernatural Christ is thus a natural necessity. It is in the supernatural mere nature must discover that reinforcement, that new birth to a higher plane, without which there never can be destiny.

And so Christ is a cosmic value because in His total impact—His life, His truth, His martyrdom, His redemptive sacrifice, His death-conquering resurrection, His continuing Church in which He remains permanently manifest—He has done something at once to life and to history. Unquestionably, He is a teacher; but He is a teacher and something more. Unquestionably, He is a martyr; but He is a martyr and something more. And it is this *more* which makes Him the one complete answer to human need. He is indeed the cosmic Christ. He is destiny made manifest in the midst of probation. He is eternity made manifest in the midst of time. He is the supreme creative resource of the Infinite operating upon personalities at the moral level rather than upon things at the mechanical level.

An analytical statement of this truth will help us to grasp it. There are four chief values:

1. Jesus Christ and His resurrection from the dead marks off a new epoch in the evolutionary increase of creation.

2. Jesus Christ, having invaded history, and having died as sinful men in nature die, had come utterly close both to men and to their sins. Consequently the judgment forth-uttered in His death was able to transform the falsehood of all sin into an expression of the truth of the holiness of God.

3. Jesus Christ standing thus near man in history, and dying on his behalf, becomes a supreme expression of the Divine love, and so woos man from his fear of the moral Infinite.

4. Jesus Christ in His risen triumph is at once the organizing center of the Kingdom of God (the social unity which fulfills man's sense of destiny) and the answer of the universe to the age-old aspirations of man's soul.

An interpretive word about each one of these immense values will be helpful.

I

First of all, then, the life, death, and resurrection of Jesus mark the beginning of a new era in the story of creation, an era as clearly discriminated as that marked by the appearance of life in the midst of the inorganic, or of moral personalities in the midst of the animal world. The Resurrection of Jesus is the historic beginning of Eternal Life within the universe. Before the Resurrection, death reigned; and dying life is both qualitatively and quantitatively different from Eternal Life.

Death was fit enough to natural life. And it was fit also, at least in part, to sinning man. But to man actually attaining his moral destiny, death is not fit. Consequently, somewhere in the stream of history Eternal Life has to be made manifest; and it has to be made manifest precisely as life, victorious over death. The resurrection of Jesus Christ is thus the first manifestation within the universe of man in his full proportions.

But immediately there will be an objection, for death did not disappear at the manifestation of Eternal Life in the resurrection of Jesus Christ from the dead. At every other era of creation, the new value was continuously manifest from the hour of its first appearing. After life appeared out of the inorganic, there was always life; and after personality appeared in the midst of the animal world, there was always personality. Our analogy, consequently, seems seriously defective, since Eternal Life is not continuously manifest from the Resurrection forward.

When one first confronts this objection, it seems almost insurmountable. Such, however, is not the case. The analogy between the Resurrection and the other epoch of cosmic history stands. The differences are necessary; and are due to the fact that man's time-transcending powers, both as an individual and as a society, make necessary a moral rather than a temporal sequence in cosmic history at the point where Eternal Life is to be revealed.

That man is in time, and yet also above time, will at once be recognized. A man can say, *I was alive yesterday; I am alive today; I expect to be alive tomorrow*, and the power to say this stands him at once in time, and yet also above time. Man is then at once temporal and supra-temporal; and what is true of him as an individual is more fully true of him as a society. Man, the society, is a race, a social solidarity, whose unity reaches all the way from the first man to Judgment Day; and it is man the society, with which God deals, and for which He plans. Consequently the manifestation of Eternal Life, when it does take place, cannot be developed as a temporal crisis, or era, but must be developed as a moral crisis. This necessity forces a peculiarity into the character of all cosmic eras beyond the appearance of man. Before man, cosmic eras could be strictly temporal crises. After man, they must be moral crises.

This circumstance alone is a sufficient explanation of the peculiarity of the Resurrection when considered as marking off a cosmic era; but there is a further and equally powerful necessity involved. Man in history is essentially a probationary being, therefore no cosmic era made manifest in history should be so revealed as to interfere with the effectiveness of man's probationary opportunity. But if the end of death had been clearly evident at the manifestation of Eternal Life in Jesus' resurrection, then the effectiveness of man's probation would have been interfered with. The reason is evident. When motives are sufficiently powerful they coerce man's finite will; with the result, that both freedom and probation are immediately suspended. And the revelation of Eternal Life in the Resurrection would have been powerful enough thus to have suspended probation had death evidently ended when Jesus conquered the grave.

Let me put it this way: In bringing finite personalities up to sonship with the Eternal Father,

God has first to guard the sovereignty of man's freedom, and then beyond this, to woo man to the choice of sonship. If the advantages of sonship become too fully evident, they will coerce man's will, destroy his freedom, and so defeat God's purpose.

The achievement of created sons is an exceedingly high adventure upon God's part. It is defeated whenever a man wills contrary to God, whenever he wills in unconsciousness of God, and whenever he is so coerced by desire that he cannot will at all. Consequently to protect the integrity of man's finite personality is God's basic care. Before men can be sons, they must be men: for the glory of sonship is essentially that conscious harmony of willing which sons know when they feel themselves deeply meaning everything the Father means.

Fronting then, all of this—the time-transcending nature both of personal man and of the race, and the need of protecting his finite will against a too coercive revelation of the Infinite—how else could God have revealed Eternal Life within the order of history than as the New Testament says He has done it?

Our conclusion, here, seems unescapable. And now if we have grasped it, the whole majestic significance of history's increase will begin to appear. From the very first manifestation of personality

God must have been revealing Himself to men.
Then from Abraham forward He constituted Israel
a redeemer nation, and the channel of an increasing
self-disclosure. At last in the fullness of time He
sent His Son to become a member of man's broken,
dying race. Jesus was born of Mary. He lived his
life of Divine Sonship under human conditions. He
died redemptively. He triumphed over death, rising gloriously from His tomb, and ascending into
heaven.

Now the climactic era of cosmic history is begun
—Eternal Life has been made manifest in history,
and within the unity of man's racial solidarity—
God's utmost purpose in creation is at last in expression.

Yes, in the Resurrection, Eternal Life is, indeed,
made manifest; and yet its manifestation is so guarded
that it never becomes coercive to finite wills. God
shows the Risen Christ not to a whole generation,
but to chosen witnesses—"He was seen of Cephas,
then of the Twelve, then of above five hundred
brethren at once."

This tested and committed group becomes the
nucleus of a witnessing movement in history—the
living Church. This worshiping community, like
man's race, is time-transcending, and so its "now"
reaches all the way from Jesus to the utmost gen-

erations of men. Forever it affirms: I was present with Him in Galilee. I stood by when He hung in agony upon the tree. I helped to lay His broken body in Golgotha's borrowed tomb. I sealed it with a stone, and saw it marked "inviolate" by the authority of the Empire. Early on the first day of the week I visited that tomb again, and beheld it open. I entered within, and found it empty. And then through forty days I saw Him, alive from the dead, glorious in Eternal Life. I was there, and saw these things; and am here, also, to witness them. Continuously from that day to this, or better, time-lessly, I proclaim Him; that through my adoring praise He may ever be manifest, unto the completing of creation, unto the salvation of men, unto the glory of God.

There is one further suggestion, concerning which I do not dogmatize, though I am convinced of its truth. Both by the authority of Scripture, and the light of human experience, I am convinced that the apparent continuance of natural death has, in fact, no significance for Christian men. Jesus on more than one occasion said that those who had become joined to Him were delivered from death's blight; and more than a quarter of a century in the pastorate, watching God's saints in their exodus, has convinced me that Jesus' words are literally true.[1]

II

But the resurrection of Jesus is more than the beginning of a new cosmic era. It is as well the climactic event in the unfolding of that Divine-human toil by which history itself is redeemed—harmonized—made one with the eternal purpose of God.

History is not as it seems to be—something which perishes behind us as a tale that is told. No, history endures. History is an eternal value. Whether or no Eternal Life does actually transcend time, as many philosophers dream, it approximates such a transcendence through the power of memory. And so all history endures to be the joy and horror of moral personalities. God's task, then, in redemption, is not merely the unifying of men in the solidarity of the Kingdom, but also the harmonizing of history. All history must at last speak His holiness; and this is as necessary to redeemed men as it is to the holy God.

In eternity every man will, as it were, wear his history. He will wear it as earth's heroes wear the

[1] Compare St. John 3:3, where the Kingdom becomes perceivable by new birth; 3:36; 4:24; 11:25-26; 14:3.

record of their battles on their breasts. And even a million years from now not one evil deed will have become a whit less awful than it was yesterday when first committed.

Imagine wearing forever the life history of a Nero, an Attila, a Robespierre! Imagine its unfading horror—a thing forever as detestable to God and all good men as it was when the shock of it first turned lips white with shame!

Imagine this; and then ask yourself whether our own self-centered choices are as markedly different from those other blacker sins as we like to tell ourselves?

There is indeed a problem here; and it would be quite beyond solution if it were not for the total fact of Christ as he stands with His history upon Him at the center of the redeemed race—Christ, who has invaded human history; who has come utterly near man in love and judgment; who has died man's death, triumphed over it; and who forever lives to be our judgment, our completeness, our glory, and our unifier.

Say it this way: History is made up of everything man has put into it—and no smallest one of the events thus put into the record can by any means disappear. But man's words and deeds are not the whole of history. There are, besides, the

words and deeds of God; and these latter have also
their immense and enduring significance. Add up,
now, God's contribution to history. There is:

The mystery of Christmas—God in flesh!

The mystery of Galilee—the light and love of His
words and deeds!

The mystery of Calvary—a Cross lifted up in
judgment over against all sin!

The mystery of the Resurrection—God's victory
over death on man's behalf!

Do you not see it? With Christ lifted up in the
midst of man's centuries, no history, no matter how
disfigured by sin, can lack meaning. No matter
what else is there, or is not there, Christ is there,
and sufficient. His cross, as judgment, transmutes
all sin's falsehood into an expression of God's
truth; and his love is so precious, that He alone,
stood in the midst of the years, makes all history
sublime.

There is another word, and it is so infinite that
one hardly dares to write it. It is that we are made
so one with Him that not only does His cross stand
over against our sins; but our own loyalties, our
sacrifices, our martyrdoms are stood beside His
cross. We are redeemed by Him; and, having
become one with Him, we even share in the glory
of His redemptive toil. As St. Paul says, we fill up

that which is behind, in our fellowship of the suf-
ferings of Christ.[2]   What a noble company they
are—those saints of our race—as they stand beside
Him! St. John and St. Paul, St. Cyprian and St.
Augustine, St. Francis and St. Thomas Aquinas,
Jerome of Prague and Martin Luther, Wesley,
Shaftesbury, and Wilberforce, Washington, Liv-
ingstone, and Lincoln, Simpson, Brooks, and Gren-
fell!   And all that they have done and suffered is
gathered up and stood beside His cross. Not, indeed, as adding to His cross; not as if addition were
either needed or possible; but He permits us to
share with Him both the cost and the devotion by
which history is redeemed and life is unified.

III

Then, once again, the Resurrection, and the
Cross as standing against its glory, are the enduring
approach of God to men. In these two values
God's love is made a perpetual gazing-stock to woo
men from their fear of the moral infinite—the holiness of the Lord God omnipotent. The Risen
Christ, who was crucified, woos men at once to the
self-surrender of repentance, and to the adventure
of trust. He woos men to come to Him as He
hangs out there in love and judgment. He woos

[2] Compare Colossians 1:24.

men to yield up to His judgment themselves and all that their lives had been. He woos men to die unto the self-centeredness of their yesterdays, that they may become new selves, and now no longer self-centered, but Christ-centered.

IV

Finally, this risen Christ, standing as He does at the center of history, His triumph marking off an epoch in creation's increase, makes answer to the age-old aspirations of man's soul like the sound of some cosmic Amen. At last, in Him, creation is complete. God's down-stooping has met man's up-reaching to become one perfect triumph, one victorious unity: and so all nature at last attains to make "one music as before, but vaster."

XIII

Therefore

Professor Edgar Brightman in his distinguished volume recently published, *A Philosophy of Religion*, makes *coherence* one of the principal tests of truth. By "coherence" he means something very much larger than consistency. To achieve the latter, a thinker is only under the necessity of bringing every detail of his thinking into agreement with itself; whereas to achieve the former, a thinker is under the necessity of developing an all-inclusive and harmonious universe of truth.

By the principle of coherence, then, there must be a working harmony which includes all the phenomena discovered in experience. Consequently the moral and spiritual nature of man, including his capacity both for religious and social relationships, must be harmonized with the various phenomena belonging to the system of physical nature; and any speculation which fails to develop such a harmony is necessarily false.

Evidently, the principle of coherence, had it been applied, would have excluded in advance all those contemporary points of view which have denied man's moral personality—our behaviorism, determinism, materialism, etc. And had this been done, the human race would have been saved many a costly experience.

Coming to the Resurrection, however, the principle of coherence not only does not exclude it in advance, but, on the contrary, makes it an advance probability. Death, in a universe which includes man's immense aspirational urge, must be seen as an abnormality. It is nothing less than a shocking incoherence. Either aspiration is abnormal, or death is abnormal, or history must discover some solution: and so the stainless life and victorious resurrection of Jesus from the dead is seen to stand as a cosmic necessity to restore coherence to the universe.

But it is not such fundamental conclusions for which now we are seeking. Rather, starting with the Resurrection, we are undertaking to move beyond it out into life itself. The Resurrection has meaning for life; and it is this meaning which at this time we seek.

The most immediate consequence of the Resurrection is of course its value as throwing light upon the life and death of Jesus of Nazareth. When we front the fact of His resurrection, we see that both

His person and His cross must take on cosmic significance. St. Paul saw the Resurrection identifying Jesus as the Son of God with power; and manifestly so stupendous a fact, as that of one definitely identified with the Infinite, yielding Himself to death on a gibbet, cannot be casually understood. Unquestionably a Jesus who could rise from the dead must have died by the will of God; and so, starting with the Resurrection, the New Testament's redemptive interpretation of the Cross becomes necessary.

But, once again, it is not even such a significant truth which now concerns us. The Danish theologian Kierkegaard invented the expression "existential thinking." He meant by it the thinking of the man who is conscious of the whole moral and aspirational necessity of his life—the thinking of the man who is self-consciously living. Our present quest is to reverse Kierkegaard's viewpoint. It is to discover the way of life he must follow who self-consciously has been thinking, and whose thought has discovered Jesus Christ alive from the dead.

Jesus of Nazareth did come forth from His sepulcher on the first Easter morning, and show Himself alive from the dead: therefore—What? The answer of the apostles, of the martyrs, of the confessors was a shout.   They said, "This is the victory which overcometh the world—our faith!" And so I have come to think of the Apostles' Creed as indeed the victory shout of the martyr church. Modern men have criticized that creed because it contains no confession of the Church's faith in brotherhood and the Kingdom of God.   The criticism, however, is not significant; for the Kingdom did not find its creative springs in men's faith in itself, but rather in their faith in Jesus Christ as crucified for sin and risen from the dead.   And in those days, when all the consequences of these two cosmic facts were powerfully felt, there was no need to stress anything else.   Men simply laid hold upon their confidence in Jesus, and His stupendous victory on their behalf; and immediately they loved each other.

You feel the power of this experience in the compassionate prayers of the martyrs for those who were hounding them to death.   Their love was neither a theory nor an ideal; it was an experience. They saw life as from a higher plane, and men as with different eyes; and so they loved. *Dying,* for them, was as if they were leaving a shack and moving into a palace; and so they could not feel bitterness toward poor shack-dwelling men and women who were the cause of their having to move. And so the inner and outer certainty of the Risen Christ became a tremendously creative social force.

One can get an experience of the creative power of the original Christian witness to the Resurrection by imagining one's self, first, in the pagan, and then, in the Christian world. Take, then, the pagan outlook, that this life is all. With such a perspective it would be impossible not to hate such human monsters as those who are now terrorizing Europe. Change, however, your perspective. Let Jesus and His victory over death press out the horizons of your universe. Begin to see those wicked men as immortal spirits, redeemed in Him, called to be sons of God; and immediately your hate will be displaced by redemptive love.

There is thus something Christianly inevitable about such incidents as St. Stephen's prayer for his murderers. He was a son of the Resurrection. He was looking into the face of his risen, living Lord. There was nothing else that he could do. If in his circumstances he had not compassioned and prayed for those tragically embittered and unhappy men, he, himself, would have been as evil as they were.

And Christian history, when it rises to its true altitude, is always like this. One of the loveliest records I know is that of the martyrdom of the

saintly layman, Jerome of Prague. And it is true!
And the more I think of it, the more clearly I see
it, as just something inevitable. Jerome was moving
in the fellowship of the living Christ; and so even
the bitterness of experiencing a cruel death could
not appear tragic to him. I see him walking down
the streets of Constance in exaltation of spirit. I
hear him shout his faith. It is the familiar Latin
formulary, The Apostles' Creed:

   "Credo in Patrem Omnipotentem. . . . ."

Having finished, he begins to sing,

> "Welcome, happy morning";
>   Age to age shall say:
> "Hell today is vanquished,
>   Heaven is won today."
> Lo! the dead is living,
>   God forevermore:
> Him, their true Creator,
>   All His works adore.
>
> Come then, true and faithful,
>   Now fulfill Thy word,
> 'Tis Thine own third morning,
>   Rise, O buried Lord!
> Show Thy face in brightness,
>   Bid the nations see,
> Bring again our daylight;
>   Day returns with Thee.

It is impossible to read such records of spiritual victory without realizing one is being confronted with a different world. Jerome was not living in or looking out upon the world those other men saw who were gathered that year at Constance. They saw the natural world—a world bounded by death. He saw the supernatural world—a world springing out of the Resurrection of Jesus Christ from the dead. And inevitably men will behave differently as they live in and look out upon the one or the other of these worlds.

And here is the ultimate criticism of our times: We have loosened our grip upon the sublimities of Jerome's outlook, and are no longer sure of the nobilities he knew. This is the reason we strive and hate and fight over perishing values. If one or two men had been thinking small thoughts, and looking out on a small universe, it would not have been so tragic. But when a majority of men saw thus, and thought thus, inevitably it meant Secularism, Communism, Naziism.

The perfect parallel is man's own physical organism. Healthy tissue makes the presence of a few disease germs unimportant. But reduce the vitality of that surrounding tissue, and then those germs become an actual menace to life. And it is just so our declining recognition of the Christian world view has made the small vision, and limited outlook, of contemporary materialism, with its this-worldly idealism, a peril to free spiritual society.

The Christian answer, however, never can be a hatred of the small-seeing men who have produced our problem. Those men have achieved success only because we first had allowed the passion of our witness to Christ to become chilled. We failed first. They succeeded second. Their false idealism never could have gotten under way, if we had lived consistent with, and put into vigorous expression, our true idealism. Put it down: *At the end of the second Christian millennium there never can be any failure that is not primarily a failure of Christian men.* The tragedy of our times is that we have lived the materialism that Communism and Naziism have now formulated. Our secularism, our naturalistic culture has argued their materialism, their limited this-worldly outlook. They have but been consistent with their philosophy. We have been inconsistent, being at once Christian and not Christian. And so we have produced unhealthy social tissue—the natural prey to intellectual disease germs.

The conclusion is unmistakable: The answer to the confusion of our times is that enlarged outlook upon life and the universe which the Resurrection of Jesus Christ first made possible. Men with the Resurrection in their hearts will find a way to adjust the modern mechanized civilization to human life. But men whose world outlook is death-bounded always will remain incapable of the miracle. The littleness of the small world view necessarily expresses itself in rivalries—individual, national, racial, class. Consequently modern men must either enlarge their life outlook or be damned —yes, damned both for today and for tomorrow: for there is no salvation either in this world or that which is to come for either the individual or the society which lives and thinks little.

Let your imagination now reconstruct that ancient scene. The Risen Christ is standing among His first believers there on a mountain in Galilee. He does not attempt any demonstration of the reality of His victory over death. His victory is too evident. What He does do is to point its conclusion for life; and that conclusion is: *Go ye, bear everywhere your witness to me, proclaiming the all-inclusiveness of my love as duty and the all-sufficiency of my saviourhood by faith: and lo, I am with you always in the boundlessness of Eternal Life.* And so the "therefore," which is concluded from the truth of the Risen Christ, is a life consummately occupied with Him; a life ceaselessly aspiring, ceaselessly triumphant; a life catholic in its inclusiveness. Any smaller viewpoint of life would be too small to be coherent with His immense significance.

The resurrection of Jesus Christ, then, stands a sure fact in the history of the race: and because it does, therefore . . . . !

Men and women of the twentieth century, the purpose we put after this "therefore" will determine whether our own individual lives are to be significant, and whether the confusion of our times is to be resolved. For the failure of the modern world is spiritual, and the failure of the modern spirit is the suffocating littleness of its death-bounded naturalism.

He is risen, then; therefore . . . . ?

And that which our daily living is filling in beyond this "therefore" is now determining both the pattern and content, both of life and of civilization for tomorrow.

HE IS RISEN!

P.T.

1942